THE
Wonders
OF
Nature

Written by Ben Hoare

Illustrated by Angela Rizza
and Daniel Long

Introduction

As far as we know, Earth is the only planet that supports life. This book celebrates some of the millions of living things that call it home, as well as the rocks, fossils, and other natural marvels that make up our world. All of them are amazing and beautiful in their own different way, from glittering gems and tiny organisms smaller than a period, to towering trees and giant sharks. This book is divided into four sections: Rocks and minerals; Microscopic life; Plants; and Animals. Together, they reveal the fantastic variety of life on Earth. Our planet is full of wonders of nature, including many we do not yet understand, and many others we have yet to discover.

Ben Hoare
Author

Contents

Elements

Elements are the basic substances from which everything is made. They can be solid, liquid, or gas, and may change between these different states.

Fossils

Fossils are rocks made from the hardened remains of dead animals and plants. Footprints, burrows, and even poop can become fossilized.

Rocks and minerals

O ur planet is a giant globe made from many different ingredients. The simplest of these are elements, such as iron and oxygen. If elements mix to form a solid material, it is called a mineral. When two or more different minerals are combined together, they create rock. Sometimes we dig up rocks and minerals from the ground to help us make things, or to be cut and polished into gleaming gemstones. This chapter will take you from basic elements to minerals—arranged by how hard they are—through rocks and, finally, to fossils.

Rocks

Rocks are mostly made from minerals. We organize them into groups, depending on how they formed. Igneous rocks are made from cooling hot, liquid rock, often from volcanoes. Sedimentary rocks form when other pieces of rock are joined together, and metamorphic rocks are made when other rocks are heated and squeezed.

Sedimentary

Igneous

Metamorphic

Minerals

There are around 5,000 types of mineral on Earth, many made from glittering crystals. We rate how hard minerals are according to the Mohs scale—the softest and easiest to scratch are at 1, and the hardest and most difficult to scratch are at 10.

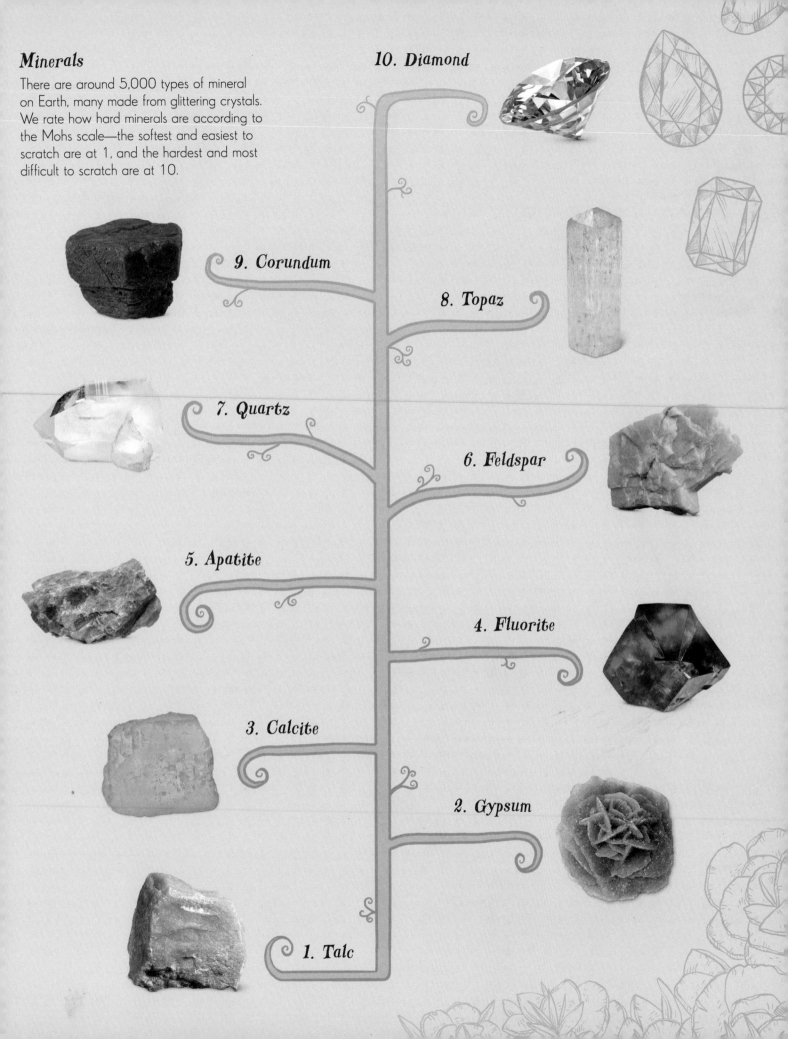

10. Diamond

9. Corundum

8. Topaz

7. Quartz

6. Feldspar

5. Apatite

4. Fluorite

3. Calcite

2. Gypsum

1. Talc

Gold

Gold, 2.5-3

Most of the gold we discover near the Earth's surface came from meteorites that smashed into our planet from outer space.

*I*f you spot a glinting speck at the bottom of a river, it might be gold. Gold is an unusual element because it can be found in solid pieces, not locked inside other rocks. It forms as delicate flakes or lumpy nuggets that are often washed into streams.

All through history, people have wanted to own this precious metal. The Inca people of South America thought that gold was the sweat of their sun god, Inti. In the 1800s, around 300,000 people raced to California to search for gold in riverbeds. Only a small number of them, however, found enough to become rich during this Gold Rush.

A variety of gypsum called selenite can form huge crystals that grow up to 39 ft (12 m) long.

Desert rose

If you could magically turn a rose into rock, it might look like this. However, the object here has nothing to do with magic. If a salty lake dries out in a hot place, it can leave behind lumps of a mineral called gypsum. Grains of sand get mixed into the gypsum, and as the sun bakes it hard clusters of curved "petals" form— a desert rose. Several desert roses can clump together to form a beautiful bouquet.

Gypsum is a very common and useful mineral. It can be added to water to make plaster, which is turned into panels for use as walls in buildings. Doctors also use plaster to create casts for broken arms and legs.

The ancient Egyptians smashed up lumps of malachite into powder to make green paint 5,000 years ago.

Malachite

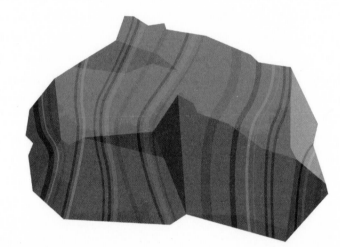

Can you guess which metal is found inside malachite (mal-a-kite)? It may seem strange, with its bright-green color, but malachite is full of brown copper. Malachite often grows in layers, which gives it a striped appearance, and it is often used as a gem.

In the 1800s, huge blocks of malachite were discovered in Russia—some pieces weighed the same as five elephants! Parts of these were used to decorate the "Malachite Room," in the Winter Palace in St. Petersburg. Today, one of the most famous malachite objects is the trophy awarded to winners of the FIFA World Cup soccer tournament, which has bands of malachite around its base.

Fluorite

Fluorite is also known
as "fluorspar."

*I*t might look like the outline of a big city, but these blocks are cubes of fluorite. Fluorite comes in many colors. It can even be more than one color within the same crystal. If you shine a special ultraviolet light on it, fluorite changes color to bright blue and seems to glow! This glowing is called fluorescence (floor-es-sense).

One special variety of fluorite is Blue John. This type of fluorite has beautiful bands of purple, white, and yellow, and it is mined in Derbyshire, UK. The ancient Romans used Blue John to make cups and other decorative items, and it is still collected today.

Fluorite, 4

Opal

There are opals on Mars!
They show up in photographs of
the surface of the red planet.

Fire opal

Precious opal

White opal

Opals are rain made solid. Sometimes, when rain drips into rock, the water carries dissolved minerals into the cracks. Very slowly, these grow into an opal, but it takes many thousands of years. Some of the liquid also remains locked inside the gem—up to one-tenth of an opal is water.

Turn an opal around in your hands and it can look like it is on fire inside. Seen from different directions, light is reflected as yellows, oranges, blues, or greens. The ancient Greeks thought that opals were the tears of Zeus, the king of the gods. After winning a battle, he wept tears of joy and as they hit the ground they became opals.

Precious opal, 5-6

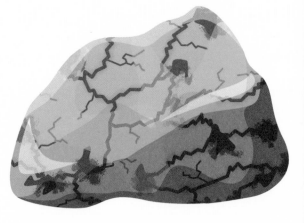

Turquoise, 5-6

Turquoise often has dark
veins of rust running
through it.

Turquoise

Greeny-blue or bluey-green? It's hard to decide, because turquoise is a mixture of both colors. The lovely blue and green in turquoise comes from two metals—copper and iron. If there is more iron, it is greener, and if there is more copper, it is bluer.

Turquoise was one of the first gems to be dug out of rocks by humans. Turquoise beads 7,000 years old have been found in the Middle East. The Aztec people of Mexico made necklaces, masks, and other objects from turquoise. They associated it with the gods, including the fire god Xiuhtecuhtli—which means "Turquoise Lord."

Pyrite

This mineral is often called "fool's gold," and you can see why! It has tricked many people hunting for treasure. Instead of getting rich, they were left disappointed, because this mineral is more common than gold and not worth much. Its real name is pyrite, and it has a shiny, metallic surface. In fact, it is made of iron metal as well as the yellow element sulfur.

Pyrite often has cube-shaped crystals. Their sides are so straight and perfect that they look as if they were made by machines. Sometimes the crystals have straight ridges running along them, which gives them the appearance of striped boxes.

In the past, shiny slices of pyrite were made into mirrors.

Corundum

Ruby   Sapphire

What twinkles like a star but is hard as stone? A gem! Gems are pieces of precious rocks and minerals that have been cut to make them sparkle. Two of the most famous gems are rubies and sapphires. Both are made of the same mineral—corundum—but tiny amounts of other chemicals change their color. Rubies are always red, and sapphires are usually blue, but they can also be other colors, including yellow, green, and orange.

The biggest and brightest gems can be very valuable. The Sunrise Ruby weighs only 0.18 oz (5 g), but it sold for more than $30 million in 2015. The Stuart Sapphire is a jumbo jewel, almost 1.5 in (4 cm) long, found in a crown belonging to the British royal family.

Corundum is extremely hard. Only one other mineral is harder—diamond.

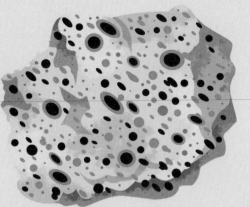

The ancient Romans mixed pumice
with other materials to make superstrong
concrete for their houses and temples.

Pumice

What's that on the water? It looks like a gray blanket on the ocean waves, but move closer and you'll see it is lots of floating rocks! This is pumice. Pumice is full of holes filled with gas, which makes it so light that it can float on water.

Where did the rocks come from though? Pumice is a volcanic glass. Sometimes, when lava erupts from a volcano it can be full of gas bubbles, like a carbonated drink. As the red-hot foam cools, it hardens into pumice, and the bubbles leave lots of little pockets. If a seabed volcano erupts, it makes pumice underwater, which floats to the surface as a pumice raft. Mystery solved!

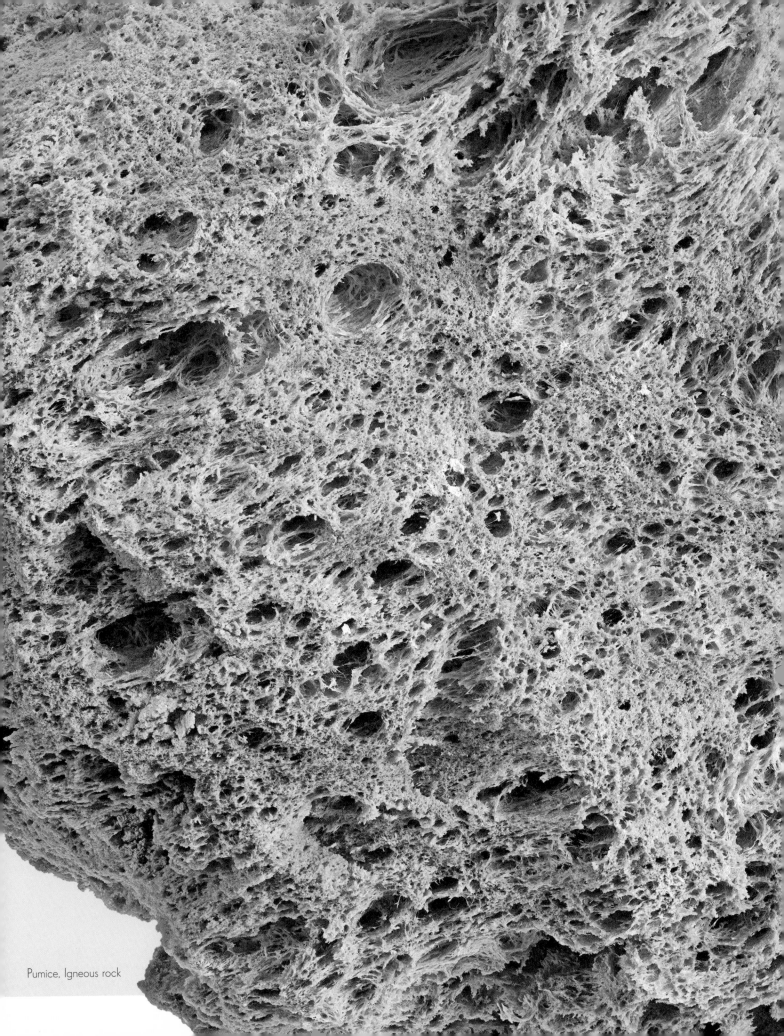

Pumice, Igneous rock

Sandstone

The remains of animals are often trapped in the layers of sandstone, so it is an excellent place to find fossils.

Sandstone,
Sedimentary rock

It's easy to spot what sandstone is made of—the grains of sand inside it are clear to see. Over time, water washes grains of other rocks into rivers, which sweep them into lakes and seas. The sand piles up, layer upon layer, like a giant sandwich. The weight of the layers above squash the ones below, until the minerals inside join together. This means sandstone won't fall apart when it gets wet, like a sandcastle will!

In the middle of Australia, rising high above the desert, is a rock called Uluru. Uluru is one big chunk of red sandstone. It is, as long as 30 football fields, but this is only the tip of a massive layer of sandstone hidden below the ground.

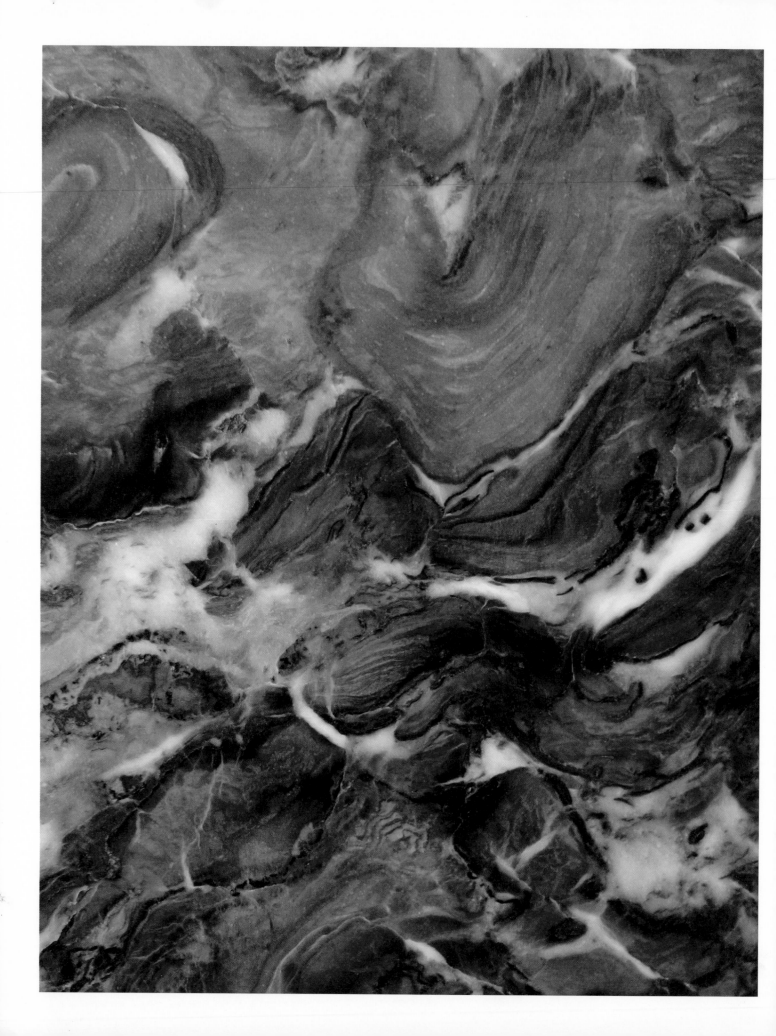

Marble

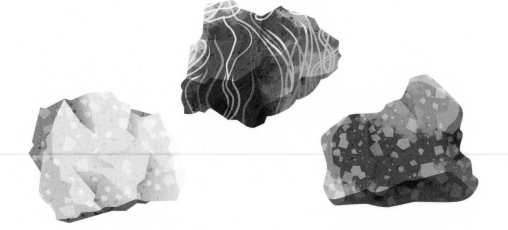

Deep in the Earth, far beneath our feet, the ground is searingly hot and under great pressure from the weight of the rock above it. So powerful are these forces, they can change rock from one type to another. They change limestone into marble.

Marble is one of the most beautiful rocks there is. It comes in many colors, including black, gray, green, and white, and it often has swirling patterns of other minerals running through it. You can polish it until it becomes supersmooth, and it's easy to carve, too. For all these reasons, marble is a popular choice for buildings and sculptures. It is heavy though—a cube of marble with sides 3 ft (1 m) long can weigh more than a rhinoceros.

One of India's most famous buildings, the Taj Mahal, is covered in white marble.

Marble,
Metamorphic rock

Ammonite,
Worldwide

In the past, people mistook dinosaur
fossils for the remains of dragons
and monsters.

Fossil

Is this an animal made from gold? Yes and no.
Sometimes, when an animal or plant dies it becomes
trapped in sticky mud or sand. The soft parts rot away,
leaving only the hard bones, shells, and stems. Over millions
of years, minerals replace the materials that the hard parts are
made from, turning them to fossils. Some fossils are made of a
gold-colored mineral called pyrite, making them shine!

Spiraling ammonites are often found as fossils. These are the swirling
shells of sea creatures that once lived all over the world. Ammonites
were related to the squishy squids and octopuses we have today, but
they had a snail-like shell for protection.

Amber

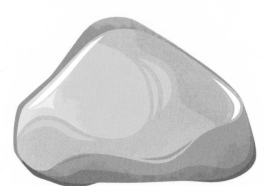

Why hat is golden like honey and shines like glass? Amber! The ancient Greeks thought it was droplets of solid sunlight. In fact, it comes from trees. Pine and fir trees ooze a thick, sticky liquid called resin if their bark is damaged. The resin drips out to plug any cuts, and then hardens. Just like a dinosaur bone, the resin can fossilize, transforming into amber.

Amber can be a time capsule to the prehistoric world. If a spider or insect walks across the golden goo when it is still sticky, it can get trapped. As the resin turns to amber, the creepy-crawly is trapped forever, and we can see it as it was millions of years ago.

One rare type of amber is orange until seen in sunlight, when it turns blue!

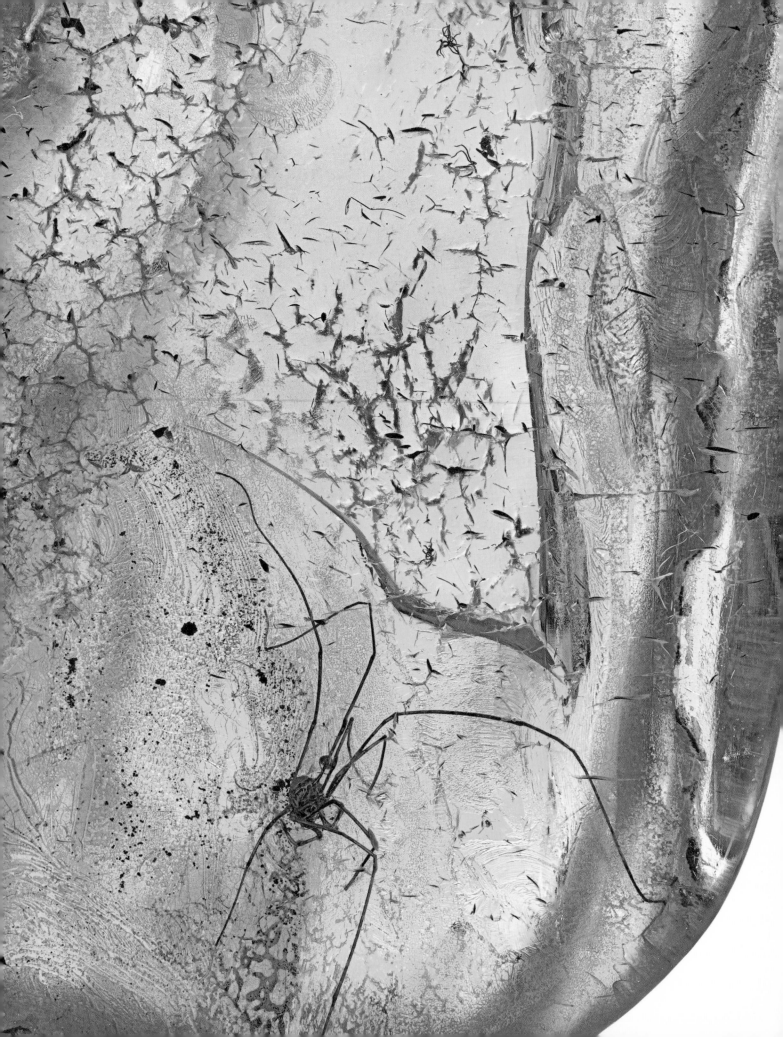

Microscopic life

It's easy to forget that many living things are too small for us to see. Some simple life-forms are so tiny they have just one cell. Cells are the building blocks of our bodies—an adult human has around 60 trillion cells! The smallest organisms only show up under microscopes. Some powerful microscopes produce images in black and white, so color is often added to make the pictures clearer. Microscopic life can include miniature animals and plants, and things that are neither, such as fungi. Follow this chapter from simple algae to tiny but complex animals.

Protozoans

These small organisms have a single cell that contains a nucleus, or "control center." They include tiny predators, such as amebas, which flow like slime.

Archaea

These tiny life-forms are very simple, yet tough. Like bacteria, they each consist of one cell, which does not have a nucleus, or "control center."

Animals

Microscopic animals live all around us—on other animals, in soil, or drifting through the ocean. Together with other ocean microlife, they create clouds of drifting plankton.

Fungi

Fungi feed on rotting or dead things, and include mushrooms, toadstools, and mold. Their bodies are made of many hairlike threads.

Plants and green algae

Plants and green algae make their own food from the energy in sunlight. Green algae are smaller than plants, but together they produce more oxygen than all of the trees on Earth.

Brown algae and relatives

Brown algae live in the sea, and many look like plants. They are closely related to miniature dinoflagellates, which swim with a tail, and diatoms, forams, radiolarians, and coccolithophores, which have tiny, beautiful skeletons.

Bacteria

Together with archaea, bacteria are the simplest of all living things. They have been on Earth for at least 3.5 billion years and occur nearly everywhere, including in human bodies.

Coccolithophore

*Chalk is made from the fossilized
remains of coccolithophores.*

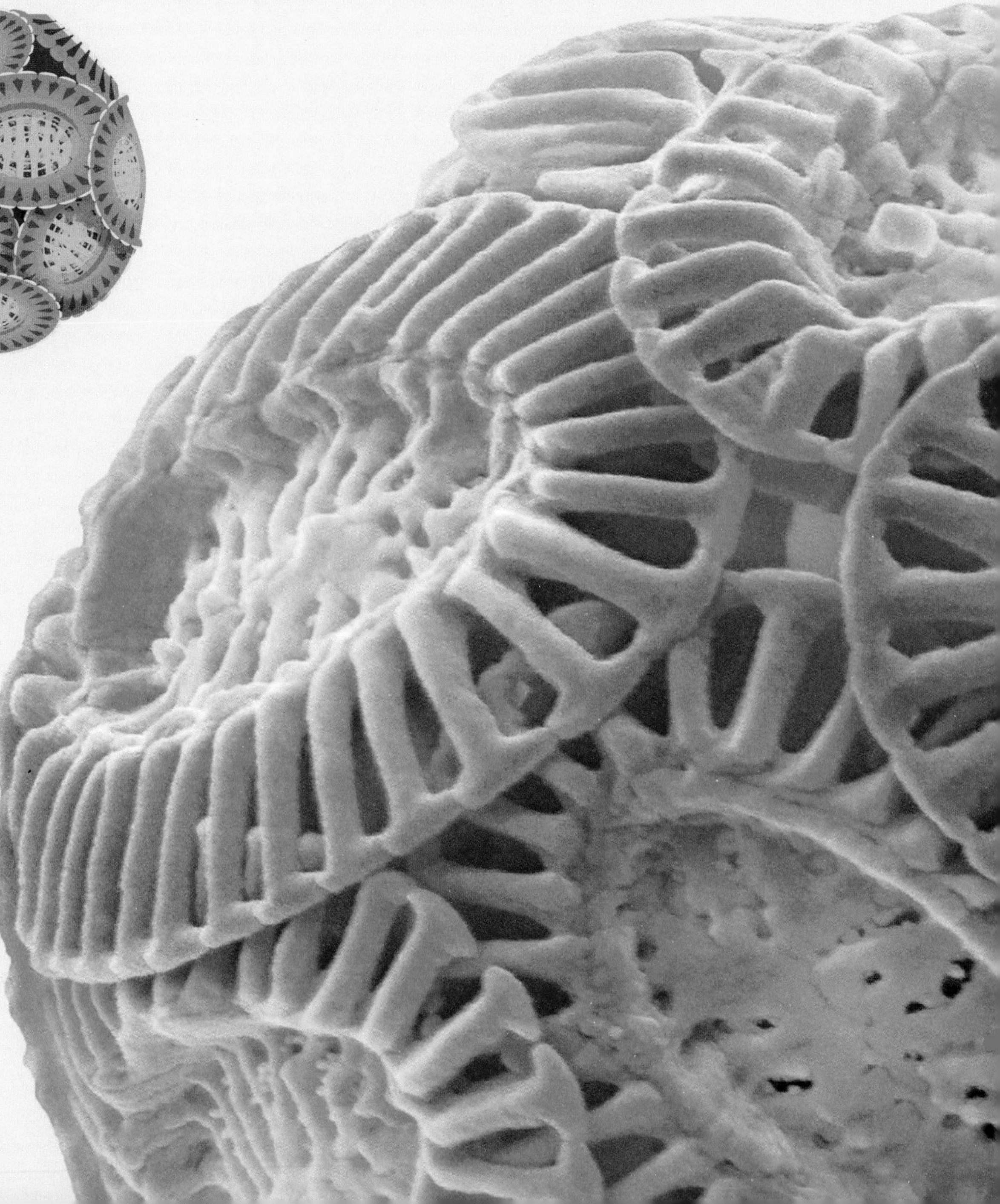

Emiliania
coccolithophore,
Worldwide

It may be smaller than a grain of salt, but this shell is one of the most beautiful in nature. It is a sphere made from many plates, called coccoliths (ko-koh-liths). Living inside is the organism that built it, a coccolithophore (ko-koh-lith-oh-for)—quite a mouthful to say!

Coccolithophores are miniature life-forms that live in the sea. If conditions are right, they can increase rapidly. They can fit a whole lifetime into one day, so they multiply very quickly! Coccolithophores gather together in "blooms," which drift on the surface of the sea. One quart of seawater may contain more than 100 million of them. The blooms are even visible in satellite images taken from space. They turn the sea milky-white because they reflect sunlight.

*Giant kelp
can grow 2 ft
(60 cm) a day and
reach 150 ft (45 m) high—
as tall as a rain-forest tree.*

Kelp

Have you ever brushed your teeth? Washed your hair? Eaten ice cream? If the answer is yes, then you have probably used kelp! An ingredient from kelp is often added to toothpaste, shampoo, and desserts. Kelp is a monster seaweed that creates underwater forests. Many animals hide among its wide ribbons, including fish, octopuses, and sea otters.

Kelp is a type of brown algae (al-gee). There are many kinds of brown algae, and not all are big—some are made of hairlike threads only a inch or so long. Like green algae, brown algae make food using sunlight. Some types have floats filled with gas, like balloons. This keeps their slimy fronds near the sea's sunny surface.

Diatom

Diatoms,
Worldwide

Diatoms produce a third
of the oxygen gas on Earth.

They might look like colorful candies, but these are tiny life-forms, called diatoms. Diatoms are related to brown algae, but they are much smaller. Many are thinner than a human hair. When we add color to photographs of them, we see how complex and different their bodies are. The outer cases are made from silica—a glassy material found in sand.

Diatoms make up a large part of the plankton that drifts cloudlike through the ocean. They provide food for all sorts of filter-feeding animals, from sponges to basking sharks. When diatoms die, their detailed skeletons sink to the bottom of the ocean and make an oozelike carpet that can be 1,650 ft (500 m) deep!

Sea sparkle

As night falls, the seashore lights up. Everywhere you look, the waves glitter and glow. This amazing effect is created by billions upon billions of living things—sea sparkles! Sea sparkles are a type of life-form, called a dinoflagellate (di-no-fla-gell-ate), which lives in water and is only one cell big. Each is so small that it could sit on a pinhead. To move through the water, it lashes a long tail from side to side, like a whip.

Sea sparkles glow when they are touched. This may scare away hungry predators, such as shrimplike copepods. The movement of waves lapping on the shore is enough to make a whole beach shine blue.

Sea sparkle, Worldwide

Scientists call the sea sparkle
"Noctiluca," which means
"night light."

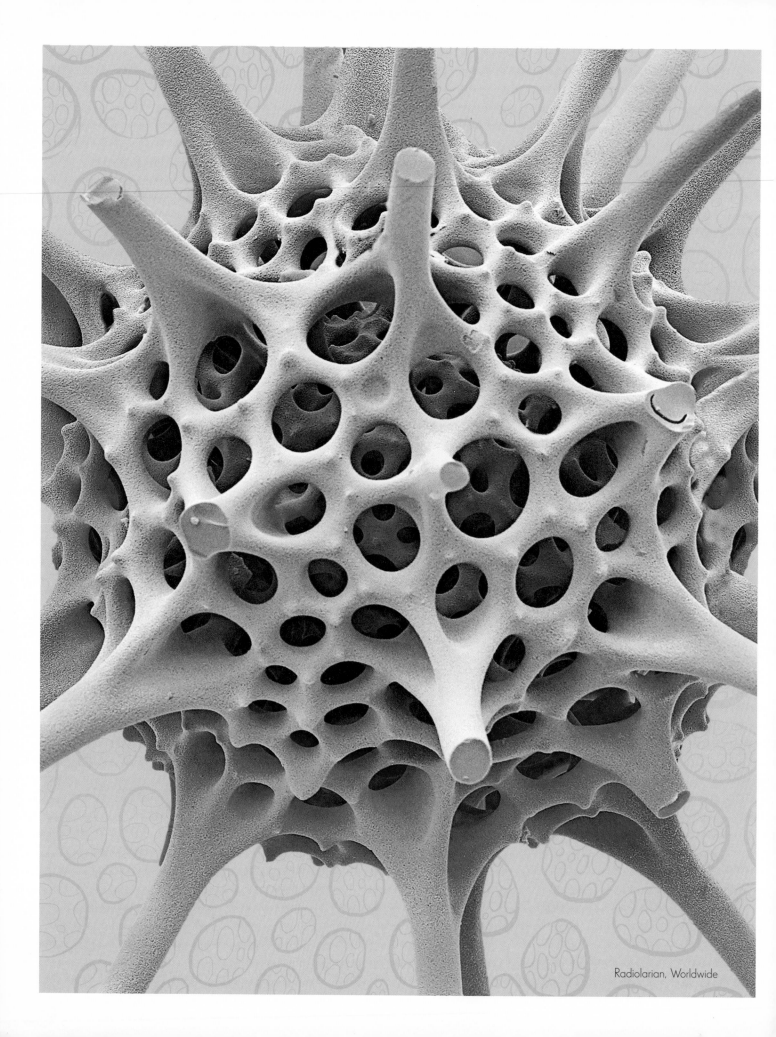

Radiolarian, Worldwide

Some radiolarians have spines that help them float in the water. The spines are delicate and easily broken though.

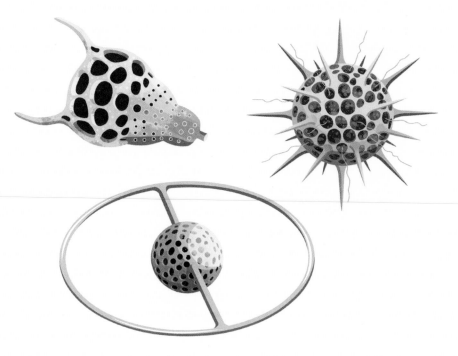

Radiolarian

The amazing shells of these microscopic life-forms look like they could be made of glass, and that's because they are! Inside each glasshouse is a soft organism called a radiolarian (ray-dee-oh-lair-ee-an). Each one of these organisms builds a delicate skeleton from silica, which is what glass is made of.

Radiolarians live in the ocean. To eat, they poke parts of their blobby bodies out of the holes in their cagelike shell to grab passing prey. When radiolarians die, their hollow frame remains. Some resemble stars, and others look like golf balls, spaceships, or even the planet Saturn. What do you think they look like?

Star sand

Could it be popcorn? Or breakfast cereal maybe? No, it is actually handfuls of star sand. This is not real sand, but the empty shells of miniature creatures known as forams. Each has a sand-sized skeleton made of chalk, some of which are star-shaped. Forams live on the ocean floor, pushing little arms out of holes in their shells to grab mini meals of bacteria or algae.

When forams die, their shells pile up on the seafloor and, over millions of years, turn into rock. Sometimes we find these shells in rocks far from the coast. This is a clue that long ago the area was probably under the ocean.

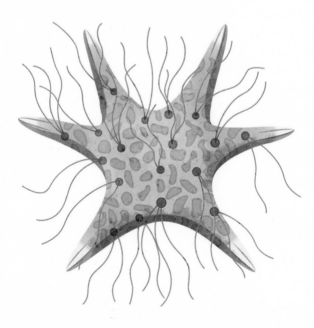

There are whole beaches of star sand. Some are bright pink!

Japanese star sand, Western Pacific Ocean

Golden volvox,
Worldwide

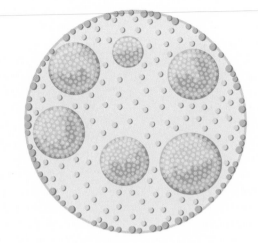

Green alga

A single drop of water could hold all of the beautiful spheres you see here. Each spotted ball is a green alga called golden volvox. They are found drifting through freshwater puddles and ponds. Green algae (al-gee) make food from the sun's energy using the same chemical as plants. This chemical, called chlorophyll (klor-ah-fill), is also what gives them their color.

Green algae are a huge group of organisms. Usually they are tiny and have a single cell—to see them, you need a microscope. However, they may live together as green slime or grow as green seaweed. Some even live on animals such as sloths and manatees, making them look green!

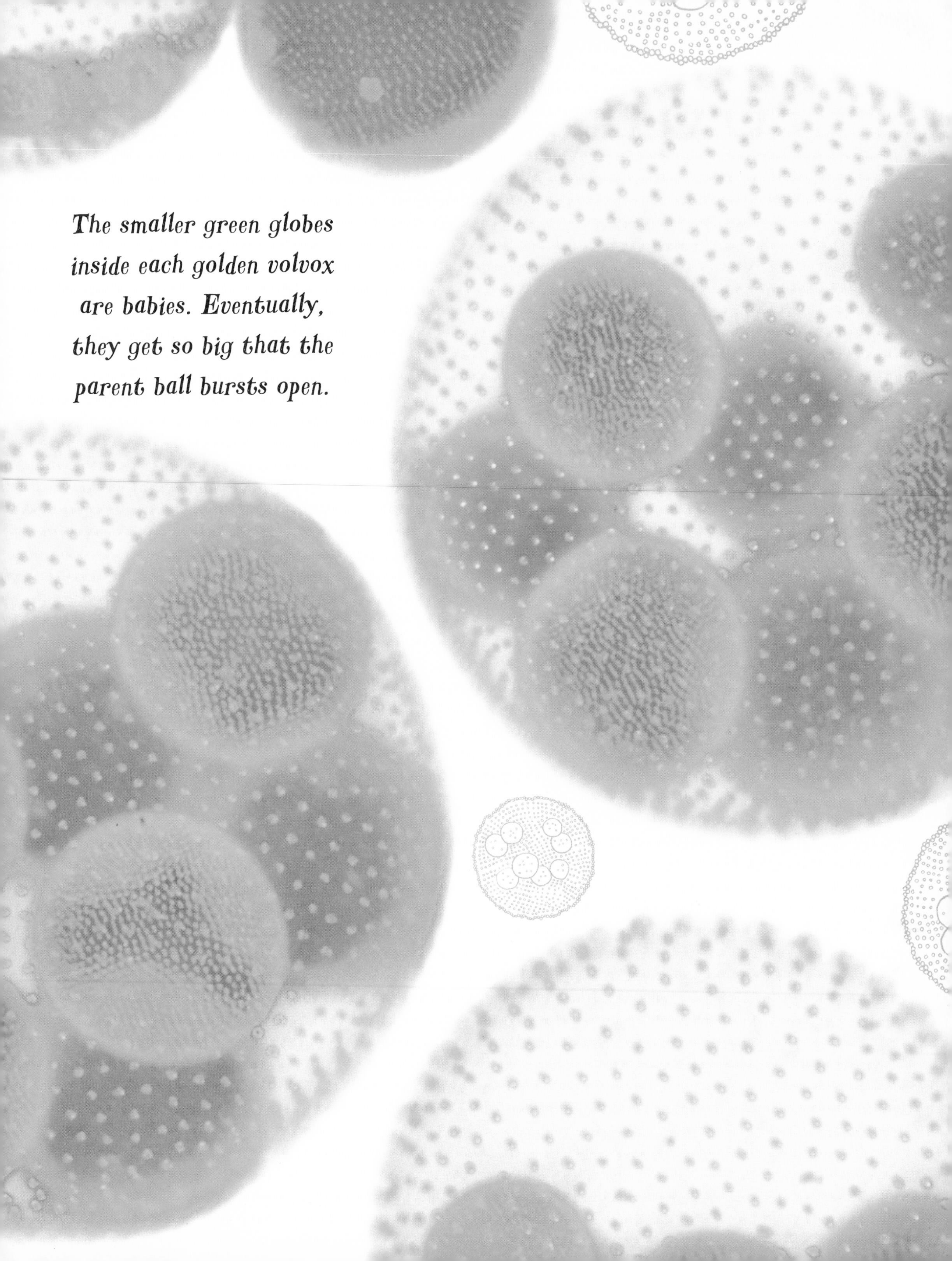

The smaller green globes
inside each golden volvox
are babies. Eventually,
they get so big that the
parent ball bursts open.

Ameba

Like a tiny blob of jelly that has come to life, an ameba (a-mee-ba) reaches out with wobbly legs to move. If you scoop pond water into a glass, you will probably catch a few amebas. Each is made of a single cell, but big ones are just about visible to us. They have no brain, and to move, they simply change shape. First, they push out gloopy fingers, then the rest of their liquid body follows, so they flow like slime.

Just because amebas are small, that does not make them gentle— they are as fierce as tigers! They flow all around their prey and fold themselves around it, digesting it alive. Luckily, their dinner of choice is other microscopic life.

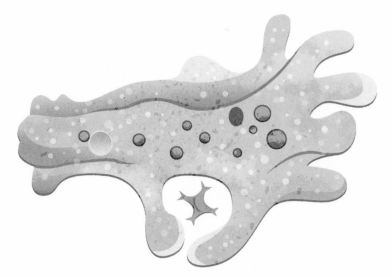

An ameba can split in half to produce a pair of identical twin children.

Proteus ameba,
Worldwide

Some toadstools grow in circles, known as "fairy rings." People used to believe they showed where fairies and elves danced.

Toadstool

The red-and-white pattern of this toadstool is a warning—it contains deadly poison! Toadstools aren't all dangerous, but many are, so you should never pick and eat them. Toadstools are not plants or animals. They belong to a group called fungi (fun-ji). Mushrooms and molds are fungi, too.

Fungi mainly live out of sight—what we see is just the "fruit" part. Underground, they grow millions of threads, similar to roots. These feed on dead and rotting things. Yuck! It sounds disgusting, but by doing it, fungi rescue food from the soil. This is such an important job that most life on our planet could not exist without fungi.

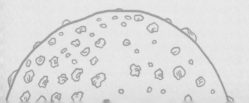

Fly agaric, Worldwide

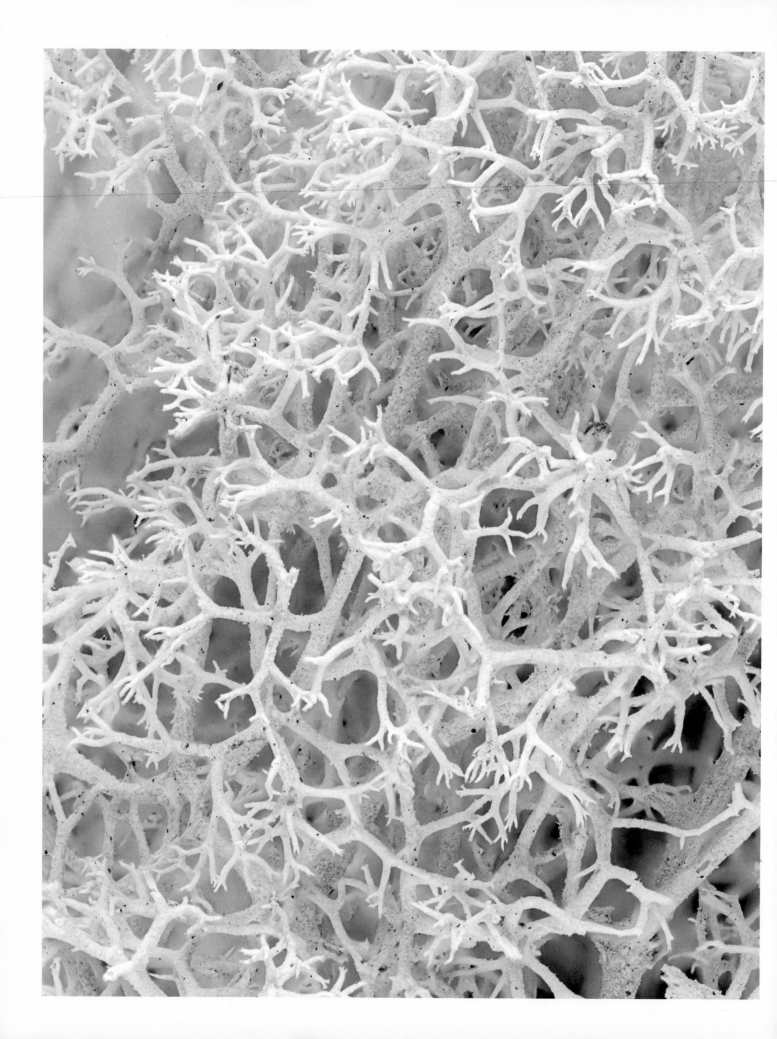

Lichen

Sometimes life is all about sharing, and that's what lichens (lie-kens) do best. A lichen is two different organisms living in the same body. One is a fungus, and inside it is a green alga. The fungus keeps the alga safe and shares water with it. The alga makes food from sunlight to share with the fungus. Both end up as winners!

Where it is too tough for plants, you will find lichens. They don't need soil, so you often see them on rocks, walls, or roofs. They can be found close to the South Pole and in the Arctic. To reproduce, lichens make blobs of dustlike spores, which spread like seeds that grow new lichens. Reindeer moss, a type of lichen, makes spores in bright-red spots.

Silvery-gray reindeer moss is an important food for caribou in the winter.

Reindeer moss,
The Arctic

Water bear, Worldwide

Water bear

There are water bears everywhere. These micro-animals live all over the world, from the tops of mountains to the depths of the oceans. All they need is a little water. Water bears are around 0.02 in (0.5 mm) long, and use their hooklike claws to scramble over soft moss. They are also known as tardigrades, and moss piglets.

Water bears are the toughest animals of all. They can be frozen, boiled, have X-rays fired at them, or be squashed under massive pressure, and they will survive. If it gets too dry, a water bear shrivels up into a small package called a tun. When it gets wet again, the water bear swells up and walks off as if nothing has happened, even years later!

*In 2007, water bears were sent into space.
They are the only animals ever to have
survived outside a spacecraft.*

Copepod

Some copepods are parasites that live on other animals. One lives on the eyeball of a shark!

A tablespoon of water is like a swimming pool to a copepod. Copepods are tiny cousins of the shrimp. They swim with a stop-start motion through the water, kicking with their hairy legs. Usually their body is see-through, but some glow blue-green in the dark. Many have a single eye in the center of their heads, just like a cyclops—scary, one-eyed giants from ancient Greek mythology.

Together, copepods make one of the greatest journeys on Earth. By the light of the moon, masses of them rise to the surface of the ocean, all over the world. Every morning, they sink back down to the depths again. This helps them to avoid hungry fish during the daytime.

Temora copepod,
Atlantic Ocean

Mosses

Mosses are simple plants that grow in round pillows or soft carpets. Most live in damp places, such as forests or near freshwater. There are more than 9,000 types of moss.

Ferns

With their coiled stems and feathered fronds, ferns are a familiar sight in the forest. Ferns, like liverworts, mosses, and club mosses, reproduce by releasing clouds of tiny spores instead of seeds.

Plants

From the smallest clumps of moss to the tallest trees, plants really do come in all shapes and sizes. Unlike animals, plants can't move around to chase other plants or animals to eat. Most make all the food they need from just three main things: water, sunlight, and carbon dioxide gas. If you imagine a plant, you probably think of the color green. This green color comes from a pigment called chlorophyll (klor-ah-fill), and it is this magical substance that traps energy from sunlight, so plants can make sugar for food. This chapter is arranged from simple liverworts all the way up to dazzling flowers.

Conifers

Conifers and their relatives are plants that produce their seeds inside cones. Common conifers, such as firs, pines, and cypresses, are often evergreen, keeping their spiked, needlelike leaves year-round.

Flowering plants

Most of the plants you see around you will belong to the flowering plants group. Many make beautiful flowers to attract pollinators—animals that move pollen from one flower to another so they can make fruit and seeds.

Club mosses

Club mosses aren't actually mosses, but are another group of primitive plants. Millions of years ago, these plants grew as tall as trees, but today, all club mosses are small. Their simple leaves are hard, narrow, and scaly.

Liverworts

At first, the Earth's land was bare and rocky. Liverworts were some of the first green plants to appear. They don't have roots, leaves, or stems, and they creep across the ground in wet habitats.

Each liverwort can grow to several yards across over many years.

Liverwort

Step back in time 470 million years and you wouldn't see any animals on the land. No dinosaurs, no mammals, not even insects. However, you would see plants—bright-green liverworts. Liverworts are simple plants that don't have any roots, veins, stems, or flowers. Without stems, they can't grow very tall. Instead, they have to creep across soil and rocks, lurking only in damp and dark places.

Occasionally, liverworts sprout what look like tiny umbrellas. These don't keep off rain though. They help the liverwort make spores—seedlike particles from which new liverworts grow. Liverworts can also reproduce from miniature copies of themselves made in little cups on their surface.

Common liverwort, Europe

Spike moss

Raindrops begin to fall on the hot, sandy desert. Soon it is pouring down. The rain splashes a dried-up ball of dead leaves. Then something magical happens. The crisp, brown plant starts to uncurl, spreads out, and turns green. The plant is coming back to life!

This plant is a type of spike moss. Spike mosses are an ancient family of plants, and this particular species is also known as a dinosaur plant. When the ground becomes too dry, the dinosaur plant's leaves curl up and the plant shuts down. However, only a few hours after getting wet, it opens up again. Part of its secret is that its leaves can bend and roll up without breaking.

A dinosaur plant can lose 95 percent of its water and still survive. It can stay as a dry ball for years.

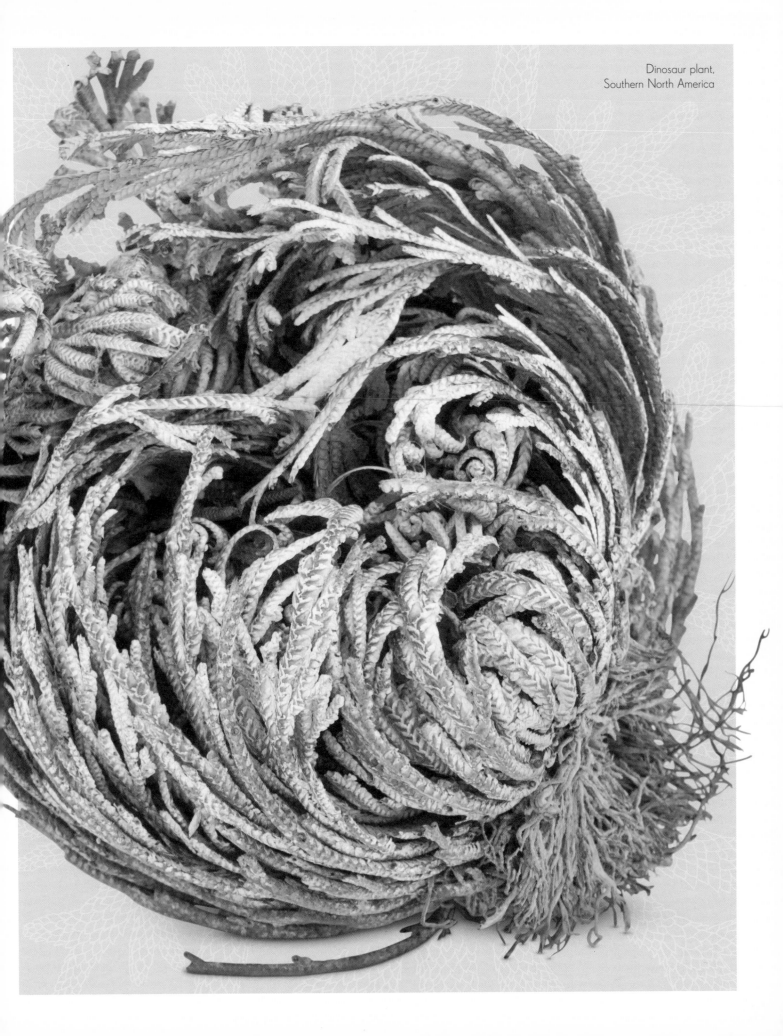

Dinosaur plant,
Southern North America

Fern

What did vegetarian dinosaurs have for breakfast, lunch, and dinner? Ferns! Most of the plants we see today did not yet exist, so ferns were often on the prehistoric menu. You still find ferns in dark, wet places all over the world, often on forest floors.

Ferns are easily recognizable from their feathery fronds. Each leaf starts in a tightly curled coil at the fern's center before unrolling into a long triangle. Some ferns grow on a "trunk" of their old roots, and these tree ferns can be very tall—the soft tree fern can grow as high as a giraffe. Other ferns grow high up on trees, to help them reach the sunlight in dense forests.

Coal is made from ancient ferns and other prehistoric plants—squashed into rock over millions of years.

Ginkgo

Ginkgo, China

The name ginkgo comes from the
Chinese for "silver apricot."

More than 200 million years ago, huge forests of ginkgos covered the land. Now, wild ginkgos only live in a small area of China, but in all that time they have barely changed. Sometimes they are called "living fossils." Their fan-shaped leaves are unlike those of any other trees on Earth today. In the fall, the leaves turn sunshine yellow before falling off.

Ginkgos are unusual in that they are either male or female, more like an animal than a plant, and they don't have flowers. Instead, female trees have sticky shoots that catch the pollen made by male trees as it drifts on the wind. The fruit that grows on the female trees smells disgusting—a bit like vomit!

Giant sequoia

Towering above all the other trees in the forest, the giant sequoia (se-kwoy-a) is hard to miss. These monster trees are nature's skyscrapers. The tallest one alive is 276 ft (84 m) high. In the US, there are some sequoias that have had tunnels carved into their trunks so vehicles can drive through them!

The giant sequoia is also known as the giant redwood because of its rusty-colored bark. This bark is thick and spongy, which helps protect the tree from forest fires. Sequoias are a type of conifer, with thin, needlelike leaves and cones filled with seeds. Despite the trees' huge size, sequoia cones are only 2 in (5 cm) wide.

There are sequoias 3,500 years old that took root when pharaohs ruled ancient Egypt.

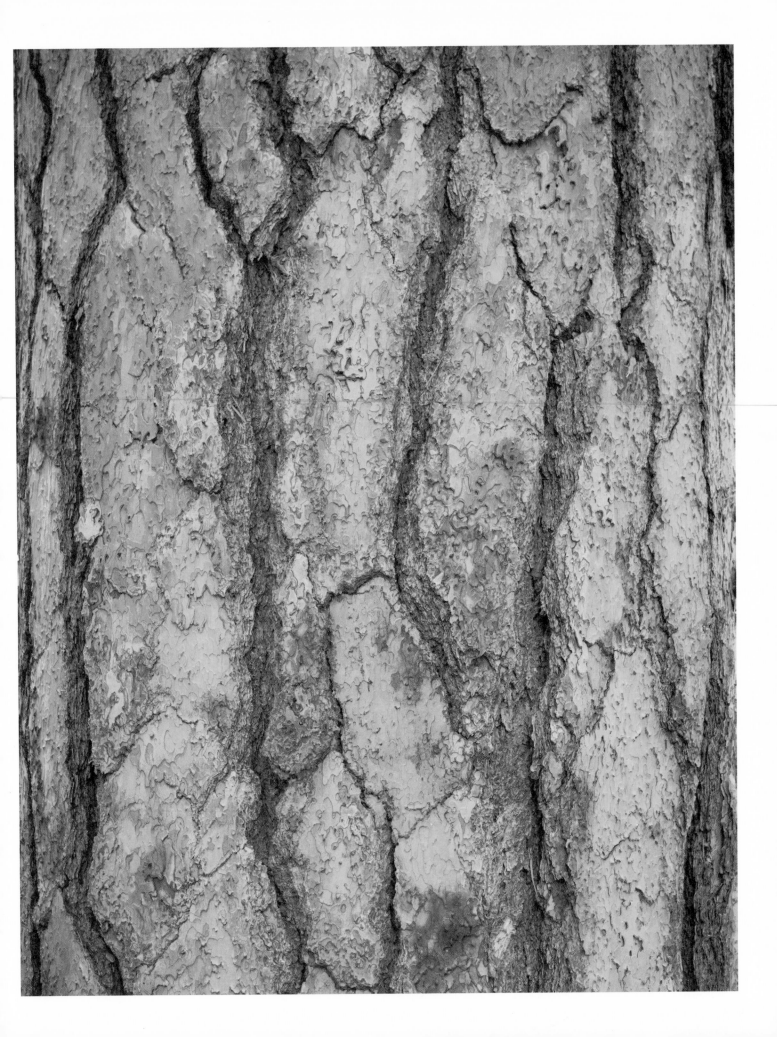

Water lily

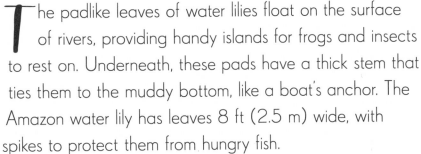

The padlike leaves of water lilies float on the surface of rivers, providing handy islands for frogs and insects to rest on. Underneath, these pads have a thick stem that ties them to the muddy bottom, like a boat's anchor. The Amazon water lily has leaves 8 ft (2.5 m) wide, with spikes to protect them from hungry fish.

The Amazon water lily also has a beautiful flower, but this is a petal prison! Beetles, attracted to the pineapple scent of the white blooms, climb inside. The flower then closes overnight, trapping them. While stuck, the crawling insects become dusted in pollen. The next day, the flower turns pink and releases the beetles, which will carry the pollen to another water lily.

Amazon water lily,
Northern South America

Each Amazon water lily can grow up to 50 enormous leaves.

Magnolias are named after French scientist Pierre Magnol, who figured out how some plants are related to each other.

Magnolia

Magnolias produced some of the first ever flowers on Earth. These ancient trees have big blooms that attract beetles. The beetles are useful pollinators, but these heavy insects are clumsy, so the magnolia's petals have to be thick and tough.

Some magnolias lose their leaves in the fall. Their flower buds have a furry jacket to keep them warm over winter. In spring, they burst into flower before their foliage grows back. Other magnolias are green all year round. Southern magnolias are evergreen trees with large, white flowers that can be 12 in (30 cm) wide! The fuzzy, alien-looking fruit they grow contains bright-red seeds, which are a treat for birds and squirrels.

Lily

Some of the world's most impressive flowers are lilies. Their sweet perfume can fill a room. The tiger lily got its name from its orange and black petals, but in Asia there is also a legend that a tiger turned into one. Lilies disappear in the winter. They spend the cold months as an onion-shaped bulb underground. Each bulb is full of food, which the lily uses to grow when warm weather returns.

In the center of a lily flower, you can see what look like tiny sausages on sticks. These are dusted in brown pollen. When an insect touches them, the pollen rubs off, and the insect flies away with it. This is how the pollen spreads from plant to plant to make seeds.

The tiger lily makes mini bulbs at the base of its leaves, which can break off and grow into new lilies.

Tiger lily, Asia

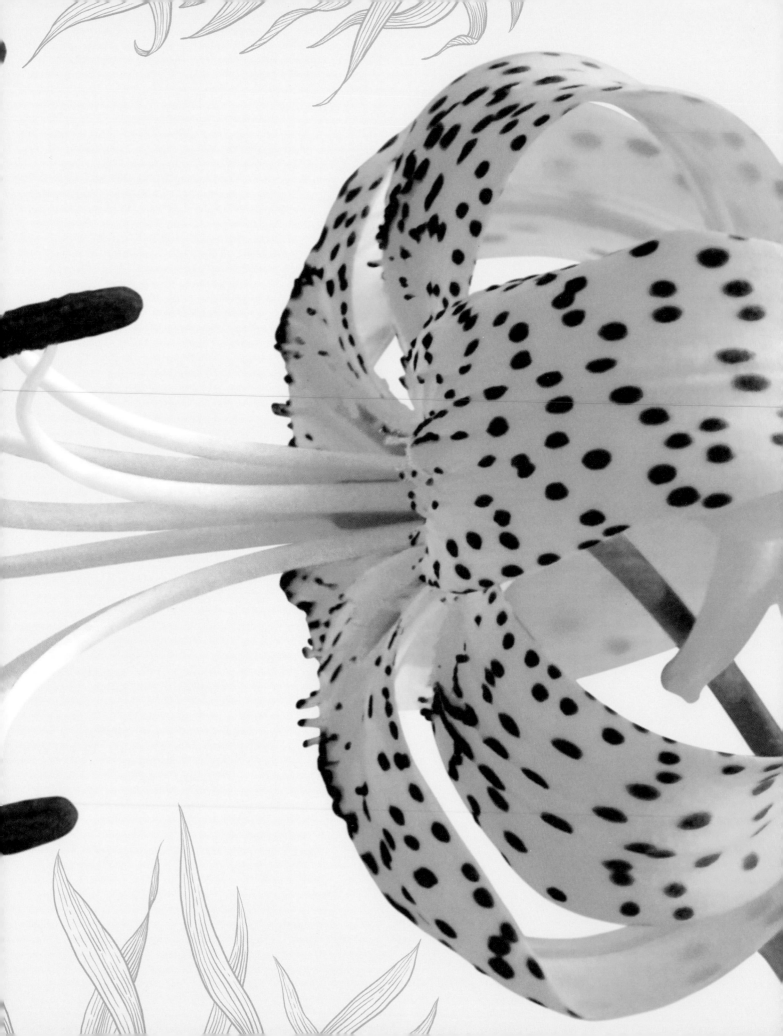

Orchid

This plant might make you look twice. It's not a flying duck. It's an orchid flower! There are 30,000 species of orchid found all over the world, and many are unusual shapes. One looks like a monkey's face, and others look like white doves, furry bees, shiny flies, and slippers!

Some orchids have strong scents— although not always nice ones. Oranges, vanilla, chocolate, and pee are just some of the things their smell reminds people of. Darwin's orchid smells strongest at night to attract a special type of moth. This moth has a tongue 12 in (30 cm) long, which it needs to reach the nectar that the orchid hides at the end of a long tube.

Orchids produce tiny, dustlike seeds, but in huge numbers. One plant can scatter 10 million seeds a year!

Large duck orchid, Australia

Iris

Huge petals in pretty colors have made irises very popular. They grow from bulbs, like daffodils and tulips, or from fat underground stems. Their showy flowers can be red, orange, yellow, blue, or purple. Many irises have lines or rows of dots on their petals that point to the center of the flower. These are landing instructions for insects. Like the lights on an airport runway, they show the animals coming in to land where the sweet nectar is.

In ancient Greece, Iris was the goddess of rainbows. One of her tasks was to carry messages for the other gods—it was said that she could fly as fast as the wind.

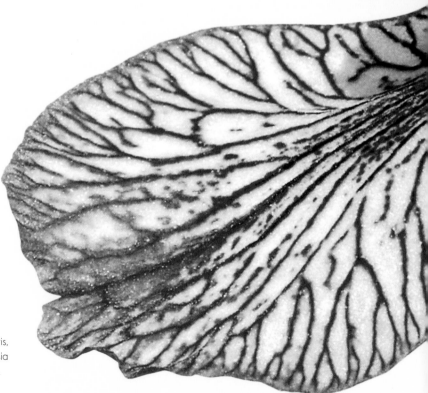

Netted iris,
Western Asia

The tiny netted iris is
only 4 in (10 cm) high,
but the blue iris can be
as tall as a pony.

Dragon's blood tree,
Socotra island off Yemen

Dragon's blood tree

On a desert island, in the bright blue sea east of Africa, is a tree that bleeds! If you cut it, a strange red liquid trickles out. This isn't really blood though—this is resin, which protects any wounds in the tree's bark. Long ago, traders who visited the island thought the resin was magic. People began to collect the "blood," and dried it to sell as a potion. It is still collected today and used as a red dye.

A legend from the island tells of a battle between a dragon and an elephant. Blood from their fight spilled onto the ground, and the dragon's blood tree grew there.

Dragon's blood trees look like umbrellas that have blown inside out. Their upturned branches catch water from sea mist.

Palm

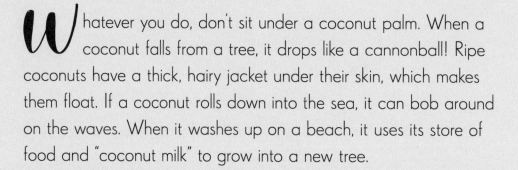

Whatever you do, don't sit under a coconut palm. When a coconut falls from a tree, it drops like a cannonball! Ripe coconuts have a thick, hairy jacket under their skin, which makes them float. If a coconut rolls down into the sea, it can bob around on the waves. When it washes up on a beach, it uses its store of food and "coconut milk" to grow into a new tree.

Gently curving palm trees conjure up images of tropical, sunny beaches in our minds, but palms don't always have an easy life. When thunderstorms roll in, the trees are battered by wind and rain. Luckily, their fringed leaves let wind blow through and a flexible trunk stops the tree from snapping.

Coconuts are very tough to crack,
but the huge robber crab has pincers
big enough to do it.

Coconut palm, Pacific and
Indian Ocean coasts

Traveler's tree

For a long time, the traveler's tree was a puzzle. Why does it hide its flowers inside tough cases and have bright-blue seeds? Then, scientists saw monkeylike lemurs breaking into the flowers to eat the sweet nectar. As they do this, pollen sticks to the lemur's fur, and when they move between trees they spread the pollen. They also eat the tree's seeds and spread them in their poop. The seeds are blue to help the lemurs spot them. The trees and lemurs help each other out.

The leaves of the traveler's tree overlap to form a huge fan. As the tree grows, its bottom leaves fall off, so the huge fan travels upward.

There is a myth that the traveler's tree's leaves always point in the same direction, so travelers can use them to find their way.

Traveler's tree,
Madagascar

Some bromeliads don't need trees to grow on—they are happy to sit on artificial structures, such as power lines.

Bromeliad

In some rain forests, there are flower gardens in the trees. The flowers are bromeliads (bro-mee-lee-ads), and they perch high up on tree trunks and branches. Their waxy leaves grow in a flowerlike cup and can be bright green, pink, or yellow. A bromeliad's actual flowers are very small and grow right in its center.

How do bromeliads live without soil? It rains a lot in tropical forests, so the plants catch all the water they need from the air. The rain even trickles into the middle of their leaves and forms small ponds. These treetop tanks are home to tadpoles of frogs that climb up to lay their eggs there, and they are also home to tiny rain-forest crabs!

Tank bromeliad, Brazil

Papyrus

Some plants are so important they helped to shape history. One is papyrus (puh-pie-rus). This is a type of grasslike plant called a sedge, with a top like a pom-pom. It loves to have its roots wet so it grows in marshes and at the edges of rivers. Here, it shoots up to be as tall as an elephant.

Around 5,000 years ago, the ancient Egyptians figured out how to use the strong fibers from papyrus stalks to make sails for their boats, as well as baskets, rope, and sandals. Most useful of all, they turned the fibers into a thick type of paper, also called papyrus. The Egyptians used it to record important information, such as medical knowledge and mathematics.

Papyrus sedge,
Africa

The world's tallest bamboo grows as high as a 10-story building.

Bamboo

Bamboo is a plant in a hurry. In fact, it's the fastest-growing plant on the planet. Some species of bamboo can grow 3 ft (1 m) in a single day! Strange as it may seem, bamboo is a type of grass, but the stems are tough and woody. Most species grow in wet forests or mountains.

Bamboo is famous as the food of giant pandas. However, we grow it as a crop, too, because it is strong and light. Bamboo has been used for thousands of years to make everything from musical instruments to buildings. Bamboo fibers are also used for cereal bowls, toothbrush handles, and can be woven into fabric for making comfy socks and pants!

Moso bamboo,
China

A poppy seed may lie in
the soil for 50 years
and still grow.

Himalayan blue
poppy, East Asia

Common poppy,
Northern Africa,
Europe, and Asia

Fire popp
Southern North Americ

Alpine poppy,
Central Europ

Poppy

Poppies can turn whole fields red. Their bright, papery petals are a common sight in meadows. Not all poppies are red though. Some are yellow, blue, orange, purple, or white. The pocket-sized Arctic poppy is one of the few plants that can grow in the far north. Its butter yellow flowers are a small splash of color in the icy Arctic.

Once poppies have flowered, they dry into fragile balls, which rattle with all the seeds inside. On windy days, the seeds fly out, spreading over the ground. They will wait until conditions are right to grow. The seeds are often brought to the soil's surface by digging, which is why poppies often pop up on construction sites and beside new roads.

Breadseed poppy,
Southern Europe

Welsh poppy,
Western Europe

Arctic poppy,
The Arctic

King protea,
South Africa

Protea

The king protea gets much of the water it needs from fog!

Flames can spread quickly through the shrubland of South Africa. Fires are so common where proteas (pro-tee-ahs) live that they have special tricks to survive. Some of them keep seeds in fireproof cases. Others, such as the king protea, have underground buds that stay safe in the ground. Even if the bushes burn to a black crisp, when the fire goes out, they start growing again.

Proteas are found mainly in South Africa. They get their name from Proteus, a sea god in ancient Greece. He could change his body into many different forms, and these dazzling flowers come in many shapes and colors, too.

Houseleek

People used to plant houseleeks on their roofs because they believed the plants protected them from lightning!

Atlantic houseleek,
Morocco

Spurred houseleek,
Europe

Cobweb houseleek,
Europe

Tenerife houseleek,
Europe

Common houseleek, Northern
Africa, Europe, and western Asia

Mountain houseleek,
Europe

These are not the leeks we eat, but you do find them in houses. You might have seen houseleeks in pots on windowsills, or in warm gardens. However, their natural habitat is rocky mountains. People love houseleeks because they are incredibly tough and easy to grow. They are a type of plant called a succulent (suck-u-lent), which have fat and squishy leaves. The plants use the leaves to store water in their dry, stony homes, so you barely need to water them!

Sometimes, houseleeks are known as "hen and chicks" because of how they spread. The houseleek multiplies by making tiny copies of itself on long stems. The parent plant in the middle is the "hen," and its babies are the "chicks."

Acacia

Ouch! These thorns are supersharp and as long as a banana. They protect the leaves of the acacia (uh-kay-shuh) tree from hungry animals. Giraffes have such long tongues that they can reach around the spines. However, some acacia trees have another defense. Their thorns have a fat base, which is home to biting ants. Any animal that tries to eat the tree is faced with the angry ants!

Acacia trees have one more secret weapon. They talk to each other! If one of them comes under attack, it releases a chemical into the air to warn trees nearby. Then, they quickly pump their leaves full of a bitter-flavored chemical, which tastes so nasty they are left alone.

Giraffes have extra-thick skin on
their tongues and lips to protect
them from acacia thorns.

Red acacia, Africa
and western Asia

Rose

A rose in bloom is hard to beat. All over the world, it is the flower of love and beauty. Roses were grown in ancient Egypt and Rome to make scented rosewater. Today, a rose festival is held every year in Bulgaria, where roses are grown to make rose oil. It takes about 2,000 petals to produce just 0.04 oz (1 g) of oil, which is used to create perfume.

Wild roses have simple white or pink flowers, and many have long stems that climb up other plants. Their sharp, backward-pointing thorns help them hook onto branches for support. Gardeners have created thousands of types of rose. These can be packed with petals and are grown for their bright colors and smell.

Dog rose, Northern Africa, Europe, and western Asia

Many fruits, such as apples, cherries, pears, peaches, and almonds, are related to roses.

Fig

Fig roots go deeper than any other tree, to find water far underground.

If you open up a fig you will see it is filled with many tiny packets of juicy pulp. What you are holding is not a single piece of fruit, but many fruits in the same skin. Each little bead contains a seed made by a different flower. For this reason, figs are known as "multiple fruits"—pineapples are like this, too.

Inside an unripe fig are lots of little flowers waiting in the dark. What for? A micro-wasp, just 0.08 in (2 mm) long. She squeezes inside to lay her eggs in safety. As she crawls around, she pollinates the flowers. Some of her young leave the fig before it ripens, but the rest are eaten by the fig!

Common fig,
Western Asia

Nettle

Ow! Touch a stinging nettle and your skin becomes red and itchy. Why is the nettle so painful? Like many plants, its leaves are juicy, so it needs a weapon to stop if from being eaten. Stinging nettles are covered in many pointed hairs. If anything touches a hair, its tip snaps off. The broken edge is sharp as a needle, and squirts out chemicals that cause pain and itching.

New Zealand is home to a monster nettle twice as tall as an adult human. This tree nettle gives such a fierce sting that it can kill some animals. Some other sneaky plants have leaves that look very similar to nettles. They don't sting, but attackers still leave them alone just in case!

Stinging nettles provide food for many types of caterpillar. The caterpillars avoid the stinging hairs.

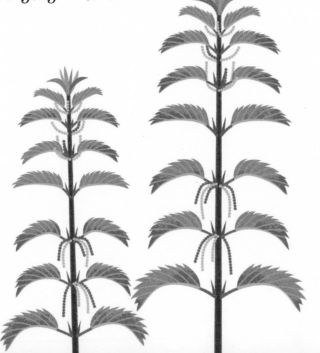

Stinging nettle, Northern Africa, Europe, and Asia

104

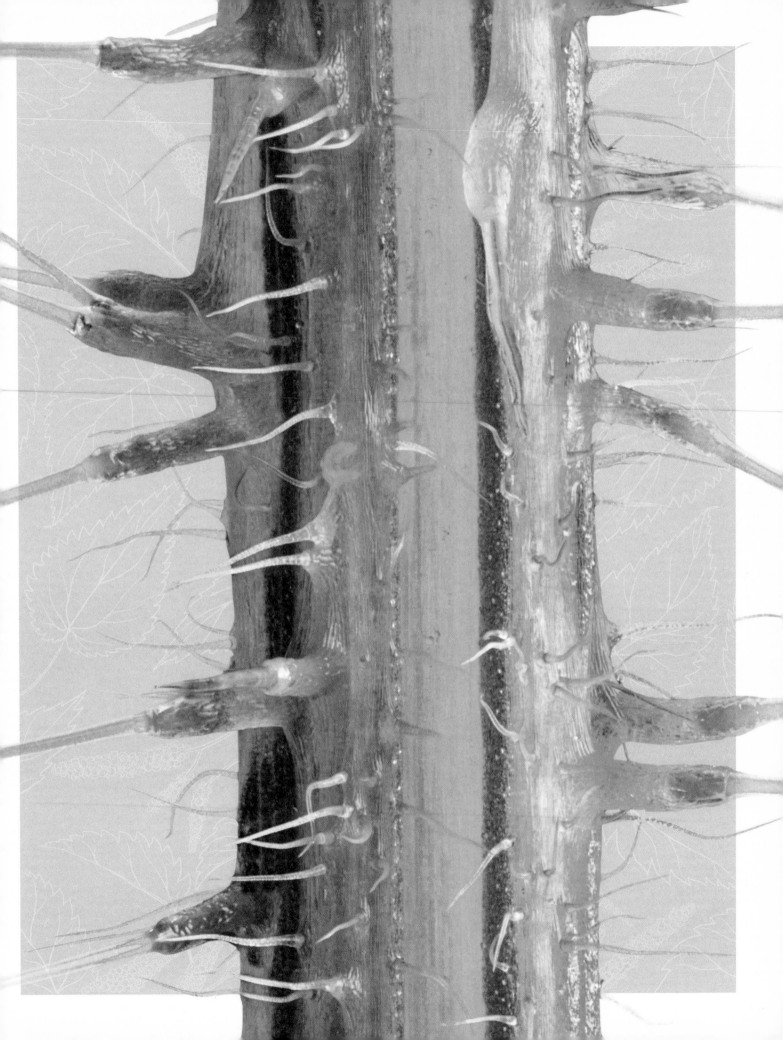

Mangrove

Red mangrove,
Worldwide tropical coasts

*I*s that a tree growing in the sea? Not many trees do that! The seawater would poison them, but mangroves have a special trick to get rid of the salt—their roots filter it out of the water so they can "drink" safely. These useful roots grow from high up on their trunk, out of the water, and they are also where the trees breathe.

Mangroves like to grow in thick, squishy mud, on coasts in warm parts of the world. When the tide goes out, they look like they are on stilts. The "stilts" are not branches, but the woody roots that keep the trees secure as the tide goes in and out.

Baby sharks and many other fish use mangrove forests as a safe nursery. Bigger predators can't wriggle into the cage of roots.

Passion flower

Giant granadilla,
South America

Plants fight all the time.
They push and shove to
get the most space and light. We don't
realize, because it happens too slowly for us to
notice. To win the battle, some plants climb over other
plants, and this is what vines such as passion flowers do.
Passion flowers are always sensing for things to grab onto. If you
speed up a video, you will see them reach for another plant, then
twirl around and around it to grip tight. If they don't find
anything to grab, their coiling tendrils twizzle
into a tight corkscrew.

Many passion flowers, such as the giant
granadilla, have amazing blooms with
colorful petals and striped fringes.
These attract insects and birds.

*Many large passion flowers are
pollinated by hummingbirds.*

Each giant corpse flower takes up to nine months to grow, but it only blooms for a few days.

Corpse flower

Luckily, this plant does not come into flower very often. Usually, we enjoy the smell of flowers... but not this time! When the five leathery petals of the corpse flower open up, the terrible stink is like a corpse, or dead body. The awful whiff attracts swarms of tiny flies, which then carry its sticky pollen to other corpse flowers. The pollen is just like human snot. Yuck!

The corpse flower lives in rain forests and is the biggest single flower on the planet. It can be 3 ft (1 m) wide and weigh as much as a turkey. Instead of having its own roots, the plant is a parasite that grows inside other rain-forest plants and steals their food.

Corpse flower, Southeast Asia

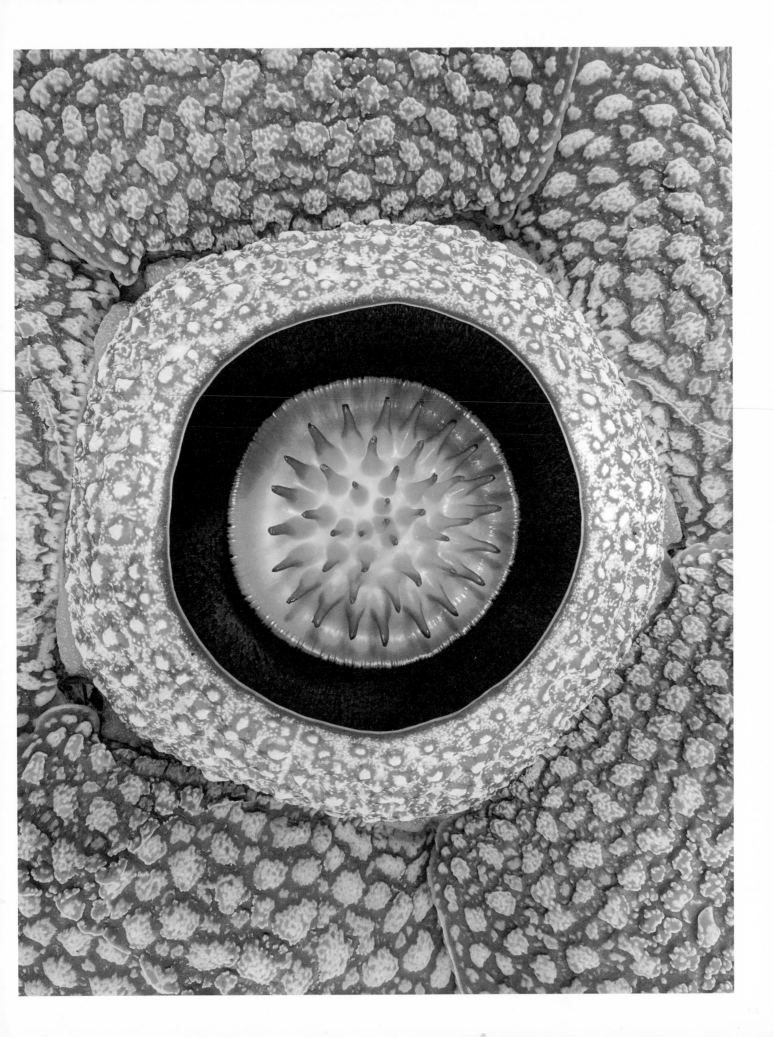

Yellow gum, Australia

Gum tree

Gum tree leaves are poisonous to many animals, but koalas eat nothing else!

Australia is a huge island, with many plants and animals found nowhere else. Gum trees, also called eucalyptus (yoo-ka-lip-tiss), are a common sight. They have long, silvery leaves that are very tough. The leaves are filled with strong-smelling oil that stops most animals from eating them. The oil fills the air and can even make it look blue when the sun is shining. The blue cloud of oil around the gum trees covering the Blue Mountains in eastern Australia give them their name.

Gum trees have colorful flowers that look like hairy tassels. The flowers turn into cup-shaped gumnuts, which contain the tree's seeds. The seeds are released as the nuts dry and turn from green to brown.

Maple

Mmm! Oatmeal and pancakes taste delicious with maple syrup. In Canada and the northeastern United States, sugar maple trees grow. In early spring, when the nights are still cold, a tube is pushed into the trunks of these trees. Out flows a golden liquid called sap. This is boiled to make sweet syrup. Canada is famous for its maple trees, and there is even a maple leaf on the country's flag.

In the fall, maple trees drop their leaves. Before this happens, they change color, and they can turn whole mountains yellow, orange, and red. The chemicals that produce this amazing display are the same ones that give carrots, egg yolks, and cherries their color.

Sugar maple,
North America

Winged maple seedpods are known as "helicopters"
because they spin to the ground.

Baobab

Grandidier's baobab
flowers are large,
white, and only last
for a day.

With their enormous trunks, baobabs (bay-oh-babs) are the fattest trees of them all. If you hold a tape measure around their middles, some are almost 165 ft (50 m) round—the same as two tennis courts end to end. Often, these trees are hundreds of years old. Their mighty trunks store water for the dry season, when little rain falls. When it is dry, the trees lose their leaves, making them look almost dead.

Many people call the baobab the "upside-down tree." Can you see why? Its branches at the top are short and tangled like roots, as if a giant has picked the tree up and planted it in the ground the wrong way up.

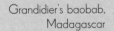

Grandidier's baobab,
Madagascar

Common sundew, North America, Europe, and Asia

The sundew tricks and eats insects as large as dragonflies and butterflies.

Sundew

Midges and flies: beware! The sundew has a deadly secret… a taste for meat. The red hairs on its leaves look pretty, but they are traps. All the hairs have a drop of clear goo on the end, and when an insect lands on them it discovers the liquid is also a sticky glue. The more the poor insect wriggles, the more stuck it becomes. Finally, it dies. The sundew rolls its leaf up, with the insect trapped inside like a sandwich filling, and digests its meal.

Sundews grow in bogs and wet ground. Here, the soil has little food in it. By capturing and eating insects, these carnivorous plants get the extra nutrients they need.

Pitcher plant

One species of bat uses pitcher plants to sleep in!

A pitcher is a container for holding liquids, which is a clue to how this strange plant feeds. Its leaves make tall tubes, with liquid in the bottom. Inside, the sides are slippery. When an insect, such as a moth, lands to drink the plant's sweet nectar, it skids and falls in. The liquid is a deadly pool that digests the meal, like the juices in our stomach. The biggest pitcher plants have traps deep enough to swallow frogs and mice. They eat everything except the skeleton!

A mouselike animal called a tree shrew visits pitcher plants to lick their nectar. Afterward, it uses the plants as a bathroom! The plants don't mind, because the shrew poop is extra food!

Tropical pitcher plant, Southeast Asia

Tumbleweed

Summer cypress,
Europe and Asia

*I*magine you are a plant. How do you spread your seeds? It is a problem all plants face, but tumbleweeds have a neat solution. After a tumbleweed dies, the entire plant curls up and dries out. Its roots snap off, leaving a spiked ball of seeds. When the wind blows, the ball spins away across the ground. Wherever it rolls, seeds are scattered.

One of the most colorful tumbleweeds is summer cypress. It turns from green to bright pink in fall, making it look like it is burning. In fact, in hot weather, heaps of dry tumbleweed are a serious fire risk because they pile up and catch fire easily.

In the United States, the wind sweeps tumbleweeds into great heaps that block roads and bury whole houses.

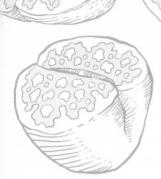

Living stones make their own sunscreen
so they don't burn in the desert sun.

Living stone

Is that a flower growing out of a rock? Living stones grow in deserts. Their round leaves do a good impression of pebbles—so good that these plants are difficult to spot among real stones. Desert animals, such as tortoises and ostriches, walk straight past the plants and miss out on a meal. Living stones are only easy to see when their single, daisylike flower blooms after rain falls.

Living stones have a single pair of chunky leaves that store water. What we see is just the leaf tips—the rest is buried underground. To get enough light to make food, the tops of the leaves have "windows" to let sunshine into the plant, which is see-through inside.

Karas Mountains
living stone,
Southern Africa

Cactus

You wouldn't want to touch a cactus by mistake. These desert plants are lined with neat rows of sharp spines. The prickly protection stops thirsty animals from getting at the water stored in their spongelike stems. The spines are actually special leaves. Big, flat leaves would lose lots of water in the hot sun. A crinkled surface helps cacti to stay cool by creating shade.

Deserts in Mexico and the US have the largest species of cactus in the world, the saguaro (sa-war-uh). Lots of animals visit it. Bats come to feed at its flowers at night, and woodpeckers peck nest holes in it. When the woodpeckers move out, tiny elf owls move in.

A saguaro cactus can reach 50 ft (15 m) tall and weigh as much as a small car.

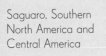

Saguaro, Southern
North America and
Central America

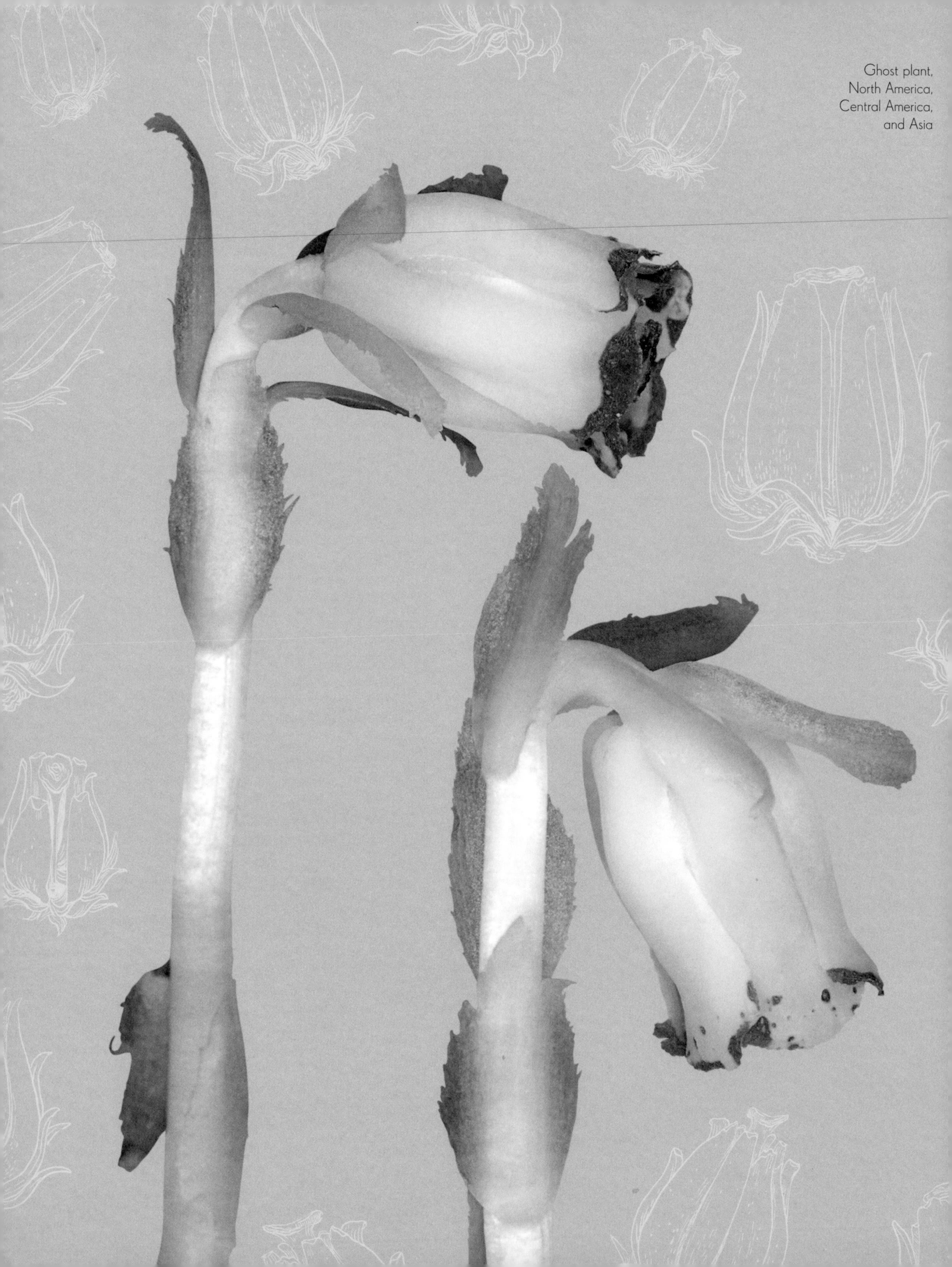

Ghost plant,
North America,
Central America,
and Asia

*Don't be tempted
to pick a ghost plant
flower. If you do,
it turns black.*

Ghost plant

Under the shade of the forest trees, among fallen leaves, is where you will find this pale plant. It is white as paper and waxy as a candle. You can almost see straight through it! Each little stem grows up to 12 in (30 cm) high and has a single, spooky flower.

Most plants capture energy from the sun and turn it into sugar for food. This is called photosynthesis (photo-sin-theh-sis), and the parts of the plant that do it are what make them green. However, the ghost plant doesn't need sunlight. So how does it get its food? It sucks up nutrients from fungi living in the ground.

Sunflower

From a small, striped seed, a mighty plant grows. The sunflower shoots up to the sky, and after only a few months it can be taller than five adult humans standing on each other's shoulders! Its golden petals form a huge ring around a dark center. This disk holds lots and lots of smaller flowers—each of which later becomes a seed.

Sunflowers grow wild in the grasslands of the US and Mexico. These are shorter and have smaller flower heads than garden sunflowers. Several thousand years ago, Native American people began to farm sunflowers for their seeds, which are tasty and can be crushed into cooking oil. Today, gardeners try to grow the tallest plants with the biggest flowers.

Sunflower buds turn to face the sun throughout the day. The open flowers face to the east.

Common sunflower, North, Central, and South America

Dandelion

*Each dandelion
seed head has 100-150
fluffy seeds.*

To gardeners, they are weeds, but to insects, they are lunch. Dandelions make nectar that butterflies, bees, and other insects love. So we should think before we dig up these yellow flowers that shine like little suns in the grass.

After flowering, a dandelion head turns into a fuzzy ball of fluff. Each seed becomes a miniature parachute. When the wind blows, the light seeds are carried away, drifting until they land on a patch of soil where they can grow into new dandelions. Some people play a game with these little puffballs. They count how many breaths it takes to blow all the seeds off them—this is supposed to tell the time. That's why they are sometimes called "dandelion clocks."

Sea holly

Sea holly stores fresh
water underground
in a fat root.

andy beaches are where you find sea holly. It is usually in the sand dunes, as it likes to shelter there, out of the wind. With blue leaves and purple flowers, sea holly is hard to miss. Being a seaside plant is not easy, because the salty air is bad for leaves and makes them dry out. Sea holly has tough, waxy leaves that keep water in.

Sea holly's jagged edges keep nibbling animals away, especially from the tight balls of flowers. All sharp and spiked, it may remind you of holly trees. However, you might be surprised to learn which family of plants it belongs to: the carrot family!

Sea holly, Europe

Birds

Can you see feathers? Then you're looking at a bird. Birds also have beaks and lay hard-shelled eggs. Most birds can fly, but some have lost the power of flight, so they walk or run.

Mammals

Fur means it's a mammal. Sea mammals often have smooth bodies, but even they have wisps of hair. All female mammals feed milk to their young. Most give birth, but a few unusual mammals lay eggs instead.

Reptiles

Hard scales are a clue that you're looking at a reptile. Most reptiles hatch from eggs, but some are born as miniature versions of their parents. Reptiles cannot make their own heat, so they depend on the sun's heat to stay warm.

Fish

Fish breathe using gills. All fish live underwater, either in fresh water or saltwater, and rarely move between the two. Sharks and rays have rough skin, but most other fish have slippery scales and feel smooth.

Animals

L ife on Earth is divided into seven kingdoms, or groups, one of which is the animals. We know more than a million species of animal, but there are likely to be millions of others we haven't found yet. Animals can't make their own food, so they have to feed on other forms of life, including plants and animals, both dead or alive. Animals live in the air, in water, on land, in soil and plants, and even on other creatures. This chapter starts with simple invertebrates and ends with complex furry, four-legged mammals.

Amphibians

An amphibian has soft, slippery skin that feels damp. Most amphibians hatch from eggs laid in fresh water and change their body shape totally to become adults. As adults, they live in fresh water, or in wet habitats on land.

Invertebrates

If an animal has no spine, or backbone, then it's an invertebrate. Invertebrates are a vast and varied group, including worms, insects, snails, spiders, crabs, corals, and many more creatures. You can find them almost everywhere on Earth.

Azure vase sponge,
The Bahamas

Sponge

At the bottom of the sea, growing on rocks and shipwrecks, you might catch sight of what at first look like very odd plants. Some of them are tube-shaped, and others look like bubble wrap, fingers, or jelly. These are actually simple animals, called sponges. They filter plankton to eat from the ocean around them by drawing water into their bodies through lots and lots of holes. These holes make sponges ideal for soaking up liquid, and some sponges are dried and used for washing dishes or in the bath!

Some types, called glass sponges, may live for 10,000 years in the cold sea under the ice of the Antarctic. That makes them some of the oldest living things on Earth.

Sponges come in all the colors of the rainbow, and some even glow like neon signs!

Coral

This colorful underwater flower is not what it seems. The blue
petals of this plant are actually parts of a tiny animal called a
coral polyp (pol-ip). Each soft-bodied polyp builds a stony skeleton
around itself. Slowly, over many years, the skeletons grow and join up,
creating a reef. At night, the reef comes alive as the polyps unfurl
their stinging tentacles to catch microscopic animals and pass them
to their central mouth.

Coral reefs are a riot of color because they are home to more fish
than any other habitat in the ocean. Starfish, sponges, octopuses,
eels, and crabs are just some of the many animals you'll find there.

**Australia's Great Barrier Reef is so big
you can see it from space.**

Portuguese man-of-war,
Worldwide tropical oceans

A man-of-war's tentacles can sting you even after it is dead.

Man-of-war

Don't touch! They might look like strings of brightly colored beads, but these are stinging tentacles. They belong to the Portuguese man-of-war. Each arm can be 33 ft (10 m) long and is loaded with powerful venom, which can kill. The man-of-war looks like a big jellyfish. It is, however, a different type of sea creature, called a siphonophore (sigh-fon-oh-four). A siphonophore is a collection of many animals sharing the same body. Each animal has a different job. Some catch prey, while others digest food or help the body float. They work together, yet none has a brain. They drift together on the ocean, wherever the wind and waves take them.

Flatworm

Tiger flatworm, Indian
and Pacific Oceans

Rippling through the water of warm oceans, the tiger flatworm hunts for tubelike sea squirts to eat. Most flatworms live in freshwater or the sea, but some also creep over the wet ground of tropical forests. Others live as parasites inside bigger animals. Their delicate skin can be brightly colored, but sometimes it is so thin that it's see-through.

Flatworms are simple animals, and they don't have a heart, lungs, blood, eyes, or even a true mouth. Their slim bodies have only one opening—where food goes in and waste comes out. However, some have an amazing survival trick. If you chop them up, the different pieces will all grow into new flatworms!

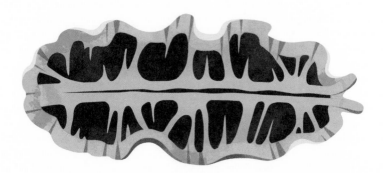

Worm

In certain parts of the ocean, it feels like Christmas every day. Here, the seabed is covered in what looks like a tiny forest of Christmas trees. These are actually colorful worms! The "branches" are crowns of feathery tentacles, which the worms use to trap scraps of food drifting past. If they are surprised, the worms quickly draw their tentacles in, and the "forest" disappears.

Christmas tree worms are part of a large group of animals, called segmented worms, whose soft bodies have many sections. Segmented worms live almost everywhere. Some live under the ice in Antarctica, others live on boiling volcanic vents in the deep sea, while trillions of earthworms are packed into our planet's soil.

Worms are full of water at high pressure, like the air in a tire.

Christmas tree worm,
Worldwide tropical oceans

Giant clam

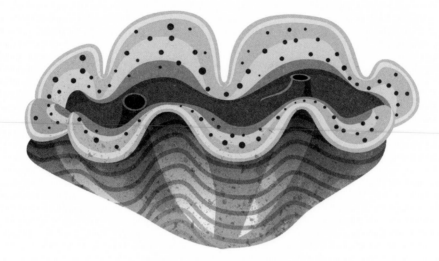

Among the rocky cracks and caves of a coral reef, you might spot a giant blue mouth. It belongs to the small giant clam. This monster mollusk is up to 16 in (40 cm) long, but it is small in comparison to the giant clam, which is the biggest shelled mollusk in the world. Giant clams can grow to 10,000 times heavier than garden snails, which are also members of the mollusk group!

Giant clams are related to mussels, scallops, and oysters, and, like them, they have a hard shell made of two hinged parts. The frilly lips yawn open during the day, allowing the sun to reach the algae living inside. The algae use the sunlight to make food, which the clam eats.

Each giant clam has several hundred eyes on its wavy lips.

Snail

A snail has not one, but
several tiny brains.

Painted snail, Eastern Cuba

A garden snail would take around three minutes to slide across these pages. This mollusk has to carry its home with it on its back—a spiraling shell that it can hide inside if danger approaches. The world's largest snail shell belongs to the huge African land snail, which is the size of a guinea pig, but some of the most colorful shells belong to the painted snail.

Snails travel on a single squishy "foot," which is actually a massive muscle. The snail ripples the muscle to push itself along. About a third of a snail's energy goes into making slime, which helps it glide smoothly along, leaving a silvery trail wherever it goes.

Nautilus

You might spot this striped surprise jetting through the ocean. The nautilus (naw-ti-liss) is a distant cousin of octopuses; however, it lives inside a beautiful shell. Poking out are up to 90 spaghetti-like tentacles that the nautilus uses to grab its favorite foods: shrimp and crabs. A nautilus uses up energy very slowly, so it only needs to eat once a month.

Like a submarine, the nautilus rises and sinks by letting gas and water in and out of chambers in its shell. It moves by squirting seawater from a special tube near its mouth, making it rock gently back and forth. It usually travels backward, shell first, so it can't see where it's going!

Chambered nautilus,
Indian and Pacific Oceans

The word nautilus comes from the ancient Greek for "sailor."

Tarantula

Tarantulas are supersized spiders. The biggest would cover a dinner plate! Unlike other spiders, they don't build webs to catch food, but hunt down large insects, frogs, and mice. Their eight hairy feet have sensors that can feel tiny vibrations made by prey.

Tarantulas are named after Taranto, a town in Italy. The people there said the only way to survive the venom from a spider bite was to do a fast dance called the Tarantella. In fact, most tarantulas are harmless to humans. Some do have a nasty defense though. Using their back legs, they scrape super-itchy hairs from their bodies and flick a cloud of them into the face of their attacker. These irritate the predator's eyes and nose.

Cobalt blue tarantula, Southeast Asia

Female tarantulas can live
as long as 35 years.

Bumblebee millipede,
Caribbean

*Millipedes are vegetarians and eat only
dead and rotting plants.*

Millipede

Around 420 million years ago, millipedes left the oceans and became some of the first creatures to walk on land. It's a good thing these creepy-crawlies don't have to get dressed in the morning, because they have more legs than any other animal. The record is 375 pairs of legs, but 50–100 pairs is more common.

The body of a millipede has many joints, so it's as flexible as a worm and can curl into a ball to protect itself. Some millipedes also release a horrid stink to put off predators. Others make a deadly poison that smells of roasted almonds but is strong enough to kill birds and burn human skin.

Like fish, lobsters breathe through gills. A lobster's gills are hidden inside its shell.

Lobster

You might be surprised to see such a hairy lobster. Reef lobsters are covered in bristles that let them sense when they are touching something, just like the hairs on your arms do. Lobsters come out at night to find prey. They use the feelers on their heads to smell and can tell the difference between a fish or worm just by its scent!

Most lobsters have a pair of huge claws. These powerful pincers don't always match. Some lobsters have one heavy claw for smashing shells and one sharp claw for cutting. When male lobsters fight, they don't use their claws though. They squirt pee at each other from under their eyes. Time to get out of the way!

Red reef lobster, Indian and Pacific Oceans

Bumblebee

A bumblebee's wing muscles work so hard
that they can be 27°F (15°C) warmer
than the rest of its body.

Buff-tailed bumblebee,
Northern Africa, Europe,
and western Asia

The first bumblebees lived high in The Himalayas, where the air is very cold, so they grew cozy fur coats. They are so good at staying warm that they can even live in the freezing Arctic. Bumblebees are incredibly active insects and can visit several thousand flowers a day. As they wind their way between blooms, their rapidly beating wings make the familiar buzzing sound that means a bumblebee is near.

When a buzzing bumblebee visits a flower it shakes itself to make pollen fall onto its hairy body. The bee sweeps the pollen into special baskets on its back legs, and takes it back to the nest for the baby bees, called larvae, to eat.

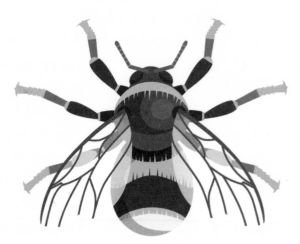

Red sea urchin,
Pacific Ocean

162

Sea urchins can detect light, yet have no eyes.
They may use their entire bodies to see!

Sea urchin

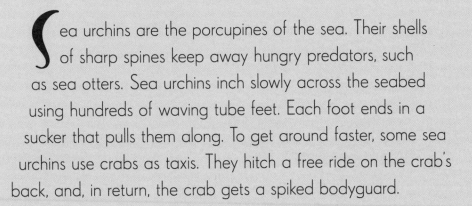

Sea urchins are the porcupines of the sea. Their shells of sharp spines keep away hungry predators, such as sea otters. Sea urchins inch slowly across the seabed using hundreds of waving tube feet. Each foot ends in a sucker that pulls them along. To get around faster, some sea urchins use crabs as taxis. They hitch a free ride on the crab's back, and, in return, the crab gets a spiked bodyguard.

If you turn a sea urchin over you will see its circular mouth. Sea urchins munch almost anything they come across, from seaweed to sponges. Sometimes, they form armies that empty the ocean floor of life, leaving only bare rock and sand.

Whale shark skin is thicker than any other animal's—it is up to 4 in (10 cm) deep.

Whale shark

Out of the ocean depths, a mighty mouth comes into view. At 5 ft (1.5 m) wide, this mouth could easily swallow a human. It won't, however, because it belongs to the whale shark—a gentle giant. Although its huge jaws have 3,000 teeth, they are tiny and useless for biting. Unlike its more carnivorous cousins, the whale shark feeds by sucking in great mouthfuls of water, then filtering out algae, fish and coral eggs, shrimp, and baby fish to eat.

This spotted shark doesn't just have a big mouth—it is the biggest fish on Earth. It grows longer than a double-decker bus and is heavier than two full-size elephants!

Whale shark,
Worldwide

Dolphins tease porcupine fish to make them inflate, seemingly just for fun.

Porcupine fish

One minute, it's a small and ordinary-looking fish. Then—whoosh—it becomes a spiked beachball! When a porcupine fish senses danger, it gulps water into its stomach, which swells up to 100 times its usual size. The prickly fish would be a painful mouthful for a hungry shark or turtle, so the predator swims off to find an easier meal. Once safe, the porcupine fish deflates like a party balloon—in fact, these animals are also sometimes called balloonfish.

Inflating uses up valuable energy, so porcupine fish hide during the day and come out at night. They comb coral reefs for crunchy crabs and spiked sea urchins to eat. A strong beak helps crush tough foods.

Longspine porcupine fish,
Worldwide tropical oceans

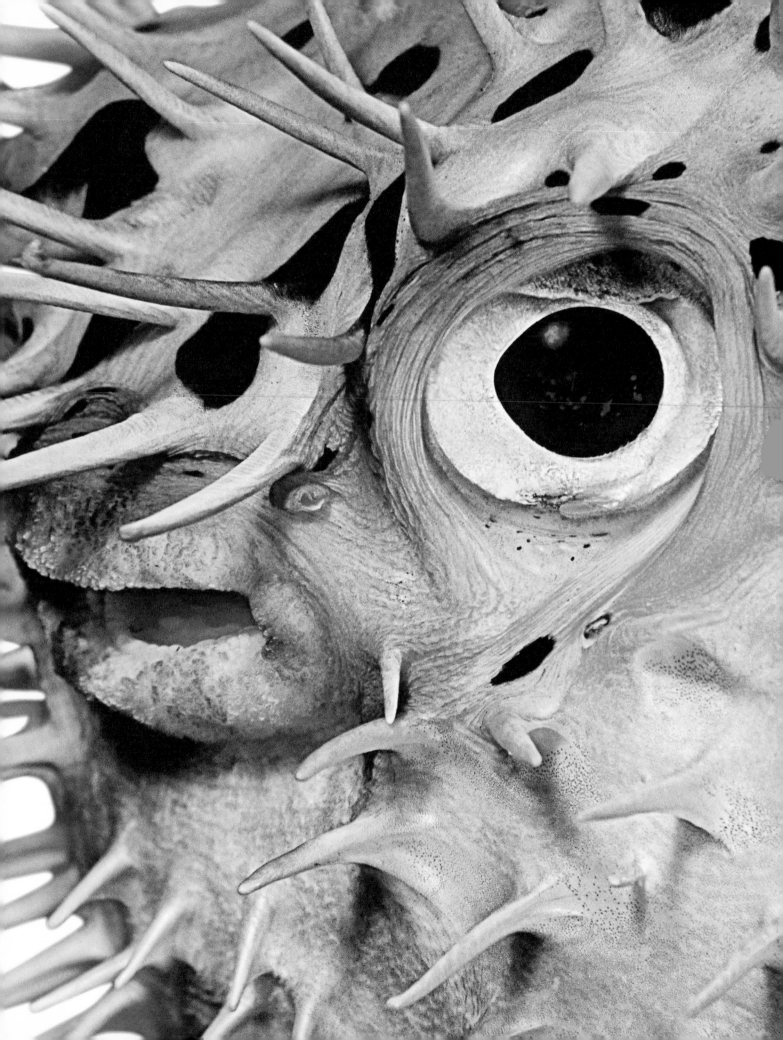

Newt

Some newts don't have lungs.
They breathe only through
their skin.

Eastern newt,
Eastern North America

Carefully stepping with one foot at a time, a newt clambers over wet leaves and moss. Young newts spend their time on land, but adult newts swim in ponds and lakes. Newts often hang still underwater, but they can dart forward to catch insects and snails by lashing their tails from side to side.

Many newts are brightly colored, but this isn't just for show. It tells predators that the newt is poisonous to eat. Eastern newts are bright red when they are young and are highly poisonous. They change color to green when they become adults. Luckily, even if a newt is attacked and loses a leg or tail, it can regrow it as many times as it needs to!

Wallace's flying frog,
Southeast Asia

Frog

Like a bright green leaf carried on a breeze, Wallace's flying frog soars through the air in Southeast Asia's tropical rain forests. It has wide, webbed feet and frilly flaps of skin along the sides of its body. These catch the wind to help the frog glide as it jumps from tree to tree. It can "fly" more than 50 ft (15 m) in one leap.

Frogs are the largest group of amphibians, and they have many extraordinary talents. Arctic wood frogs almost completely freeze in winter; the coqui frog's calls are as loud as a passing train; and the tadpole of the shrinking frog grows to 10 in (25 cm) long—four times bigger than the frog it becomes!

Flying frogs release a liquid and whip it into a foam nest, like meringue, with their legs. This keeps their eggs safe.

Terrapin

Imagine wearing a suit of armor that you could never take off! Turtles spend their whole lives in the same smooth, snug shell, which keeps getting bigger as they grow. Their backbones and ribs have even become part of the sturdy shield. In some Native American myths, the whole world is held up on the back of a giant cosmic turtle.

Freshwater turtles are sometimes called terrapins. They are equally happy in water or on land, and love sunbathing to warm up. The false map turtle is a freshwater turtle named after the squiggly lines on its shell. These lines look a little like the looping curves that show height on maps.

False map turtle, US

Equatorial anole,
Northwest South America

The biggest lizard is the Komodo dragon, which can grow up to 10 ft (3 m) long.

Lizard

At first, the equatorial anole looks like any other lizard. However, when a male is trying to get a female's attention, he unfolds a large flap of skin under his chin in a flash of glittering color. This throat "flag" can also be used to warn other lizards to stay away. Some male anoles do push-ups in the morning and evening to show off their strength, too.

Lizards send messages in all sorts of ways. Chameleons change colors to show their mood, while bearded dragons lift a front leg to wave. Frilled lizards open out an umbrellalike fold of skin around their necks to make themselves look bigger and to tell predators to leave them alone!

Rattlesnake

You might be confused to hear the sound of a maraca shaking in the desert, but this isn't a musical instrument you're hearing. If you step too close to a rattlesnake, it lifts and shakes its tail to make a buzzing sound. Rings of dead skin at the tip rattle as they knock against each other. This unsettling noise is a warning—it tells you the rattlesnake has powerful venom and wants to be left alone.

If an enemy doesn't listen to its threat, a rattlesnake bends its body into an S-shape, ready to strike. Inside its mouth are two long fangs filled with venom. The eastern diamondback rattlesnake is North America's most deadly snake.

We have 33 bones
in our backs, but a
rattlesnake has more
than 200!

Eastern diamondback
rattlesnake, Southeastern US

Gharial

Crocodiles have been on Earth for 80 million years and are great survivors. Unlike other crocodiles, the gharial (gar-ee-al) has no interest in catching birds or mammals. It only eats fish. Its long, thin jaws are lined with more than 100 sharp teeth. With a sudden snap, it grabs its slippery supper and gulps it down whole.

The gharial's tail has a row of huge plates along the top. A reptile cannot shiver or sweat, so these plates help the gharial warm up and cool down by absorbing heat from the sun. Big male gharials also have a strange lump on the end of their noses. This helps them make loud buzzes and hisses to impress females.

Gharial, Southern Asia

Male gharials are super-dads
that carry hundreds of tiny
babies on their backs.

Cassowary

Cassowaries lay huge, green eggs. Unlike many other birds, the males look after them.

It's easy to remember that birds evolved from dinosaurs when you spot the prehistoric-looking cassowary. This big bird is the second heaviest on Earth, after the ostrich, and like the ostrich, it can't fly. The cassowary is a shy animal that wanders around alone through its rain-forest home. However, it can be dangerous when defending itself. Powerful legs and sharp talons 4 in (10 cm) long can deliver a deadly kick.

Cassowaries have a tough helmet on the top of their heads called a casque (kask). Could this help the bird to hear? Does it show other cassowaries who's stronger? Perhaps it is for barging through the thick foliage of the forest. No one knows!

Southern cassowary,
Southeast Asia and Australia

Duck

Quack! Most of us would recognize the call of a mallard, the world's most common duck. However, not all ducks quack. Some species whistle, while others wail, squeak, coo, or even bark! Ducks live almost everywhere—the king eider even lives in the freezing Arctic. This tough duck dives into the chilly sea to hunt for clams. The male king eider is multicolored, but, like most types of duck, the female is brown. The duller colors help her hide when she is nesting on the ground.

Although ducks walk with a clumsy waddle, they are champion fliers. Powerful wing muscles help them take off and speed up rapidly. The red-breasted merganser can fly at more than 100 mph (160 kph).

King eider,
The Arctic

Female ducks sometimes
lay their eggs in each
other's nests. One redhead
duck was found sitting
on 87 eggs!

Victoria crowned
pigeon, Northern
New Guinea

Parent pigeons feed their chicks on a special kind of "milk" that they make in their throats.

Pigeon

Streets, train stations, parks—they are often packed with flocks of squabbling pigeons. The most widespread pigeon, found in cities across the world, is the gray rock dove. However, pigeons come in a beautiful array of colors and patterns. The Victoria crowned pigeon has an elegant headdress of white-tipped, blue feathers that looks like it could be part of a peacock's tail.

Pigeons were some of the first birds to be tamed and kept by people, around 10,000 years ago. These clever creatures know how to find their way home over impressively long distances. For this reason, people have used carrier pigeons to deliver letters since ancient Roman times.

Heron

Black heron, Africa

Herons always swallow fish headfirst,
so the fins don't stick in their throat.

Is that a bird? Or an umbrella? You can see why people call the black heron the "umbrella bird"! When fishing, it stretches its wings over its head and disappears under the feathery canopy. This might make it easier to spot fish underwater, or possibly the heron is making a patch of cool shade that attracts unlucky fish wanting to escape the hot sun.

Herons are excellent fishers. The green heron has its own neat trick. Like humans who go fishing, it uses bait. It drops a small object on the water, such as a stick, nut, feather, or insect, and fish come to the surface for a closer look. Then… snap! The heron swallows its meal down in one gulp.

Eagle

Pairs of bald eagles keep the same nest over many years. They keep adding to it, and some are 13 ft (4 m) tall.

Bald eagle,
North America

Eagles are some of the largest, most powerful birds of prey, with a wingspan of up to 8 ft (2.5 m). They are skillful hunters and can kill animals that are much heavier than they are. In the Arctic, golden eagles sometimes bring down reindeer, and the harpy eagle of Central and South America uses its long claws to snatch monkeys from the rain-forest treetops.

The bald eagle is the national bird of the United States. These eagles swoop down over rivers to catch fish, especially salmon. They carry away their glittering prizes in curved talons, which can be longer than a grizzly bear's. In Viking myths, an eagle sat at the top of the world and created the winds by beating its wings.

Southern masked weaver, Southern Africa

Weaverbird

Female   Male

Meet one of the world's most amazing animal architects. The crafty male weaverbird knows just how to stop snakes from reaching his nest. He ties a long blade of grass onto a thin branch, twists it into a loop, then weaves more grass around it in an action like braiding hair. After five days' work, he's built a woven, snake-proof basket using just his beak and two feet. Now that's impressive!

There are many species of weaverbird, all with their own nest design. Sociable weavers live in groups, and share a giant nest of twigs and straw. This weaver village can be 20 ft (6 m) long and be home to 100 families!

Female weaverbirds tug at nests to test which are strongest. Flimsy ones won't get used.

Echidnas have no teeth. They lap up insects and worms with their super-sticky tongues.

Echidna

If you found an egg the size of a grape, you might wonder if a bird or reptile was going to hatch from it, and you might be surprised to see a mammal pop out! The curious echidna (eh-kid-na) is one of only two types of mammal to lay eggs—the other is the platypus. A mother echidna lays a single egg with a leathery shell and keeps it warm in a pouch on her belly. Ten days later, a baby, called a puggle, hatches.

The short-beaked echidna has a jacket of spines that keeps predators from attacking it while it looks for food. It uses its strong claws to dig for its favorite tasty treats—ants and termites.

Short-beaked echidna,
New Guinea and Australia

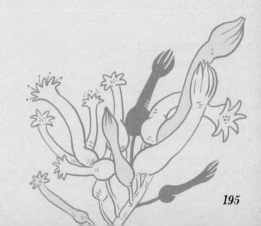

195

The wombat is the only animal in the world that produces cube-shaped poop.

Wombat

A wombat looks like it could be half-bear and half-rabbit. However, this unusual Australian mammal is actually a relative of kangaroos and koalas. It is very furry, very pudgy, and very good at digging. The sturdy wombat's body is perfectly built for fast tunneling, with muscular legs and strong claws. If it senses danger, it will run to its burrow and use its tough behind to block the entrance so hungry predators can't get at it.

A mother wombat keeps her baby safe in a pouch on her stomach. Unlike its kangaroo cousins, the wombat's pouch faces its rear. This is so it doesn't fill up with soil when the wombat is digging!

Brazilian three-banded
armadillo, Brazil

The smallest species of armadillo is the pink fairy armadillo. It is only about half the length of a pencil.

Armadillo

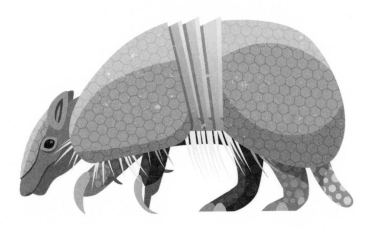

At first it might look like an oddly shaped soccer ball, but if you get closer you will see that this is the honeycomb-like shell of a three-banded armadillo. If a jaguar or bird of prey tries to attack, it rolls into a tight ball. The Brazilian three-banded armadillo is one of only two armadillos that can roll into a perfect sphere. The three narrow bands around its middle help its bony shell to bend. When it senses the danger is gone, the animal uncurls and trots off to find food or to sleep. Armadillos often sleep 16 hours a day! Although they have a heavy shell, some armadillos are remarkably good swimmers. They swallow air to help them float as they paddle.

Manatee

Manatees are gentle, roly-poly mammals with wide flippers and giant noses. They cruise slowly along rivers, swamps, and seashores, nibbling seagrass in underwater meadows for up to eight hours a day. As manatees digest their meals they produce lots of gas, which makes them blow up like balloons. Luckily, they have massive, heavy bones to weigh them down, or they wouldn't be able to sink below the surface.

In 1493, the explorer Christopher Columbus saw some strange animals swimming off the coast of North America. They were manatees, but he thought they were mermaids! Many other sailors have also mistaken manatees for these mythical creatures.

Manatees are not a type of whale, dolphin, or seal.
They are more closely related to elephants.

West Indian manatee,
Caribbean and northern
coast of South America

Chimps use around 30 different plants as medicine for problems such as upset stomachs.

Chimpanzee

Chimpanzees are the animals most closely related to humans. We both belong to the same family, the great apes, which also includes bonobos, gorillas, and orangutans. Chimps live together in noisy groups of around 30 members. They smile, laugh, fight, scream, play together, and form strong friendships.

Chimpanzees are very intelligent. They were the first animals that scientists saw using tools. Some chimps have learned to crack open nuts with rocks, and others fish insects out of holes in trees with sharp sticks. Some even pick up moss to use as sponges to drink from. Not all chimps have these skills though—baby chimps must learn by watching the adults around them.

Bat

Think how hard it must be to fly fast in the dark. Insect-eating bats, such as the long-eared myotis, have expert skills so they can zip around at night without bumping into things! They make lots of high-pitched squeaks that bounce off trees, buildings, and other objects as echoes. The bats listen for the echoes to create "sound pictures" in their brains. This technique of echolocation lets them track down tasty moths to eat.

In many spooky stories humanlike monsters called vampires drink blood and can transform into bats to fly. There are a few species of bats that drink blood, but they live in rain forests and mainly feed from piglike tapirs or farm animals. Bats are the only mammals that are able to fly.

Long-eared myotis,
Western North America

Bats are like furry weather-forecasters—they sense tiny changes in air pressure that tell them what the weather will be like.

Jaguar

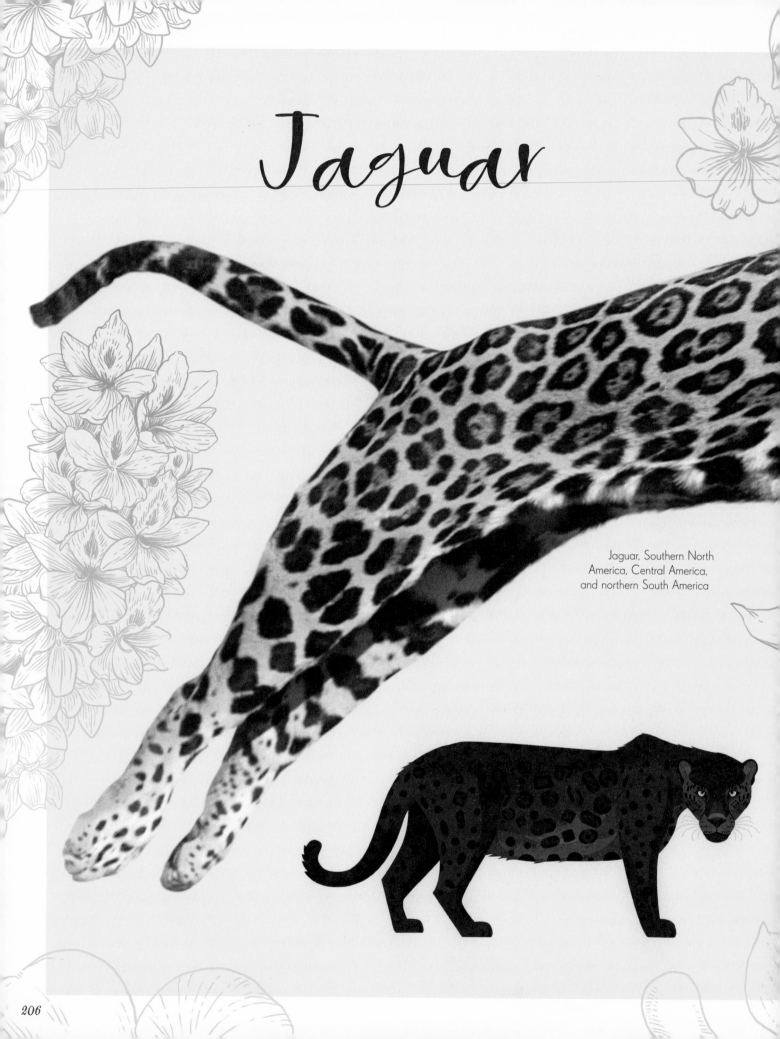

Jaguar, Southern North
America, Central America,
and northern South America

Jaguars roar, but like all big cats they can't purr.
They also make a sound like someone sawing wood!

What is one of the best ways not to be spotted in a forest? Surprisingly, it's to have lots of spots! The beautiful pattern on a jaguar's coat helps it to disappear in the patches of light in its forest home. Rare dark jaguars look almost black, although they still have spots. They are sometimes called black panthers.

Jaguars sneak up on wild pigs, deer, fish, turtles, and anything else they can find to eat. Big jaguars will even take on crocodile-like caimans. The Aztec people, who lived in what is now Mexico, had a group of top soldiers called "jaguar warriors." They wore jaguar skins to make themselves look like the big cats.

*In some parts of the world, during winter,
a sleeping bear does not eat, drink, or go
to the bathroom for seven months.*

Brown bear

Full of mischief, bear cubs are playful little explorers. Their lives begin underground in a cozy den, dug out by their mother and lined with soft leaves. They stay there with their sleeping mother throughout the freezing winter. The pink newborns are tiny, but they can grow to be 500 times bigger as adults. That would be like a human baby growing to the size of a hippo!

In spring, mother and cubs all climb out of the den to look for food. Brown bears have sharp teeth for tearing meat, but they eat almost anything, especially fresh plant-shoots and juicy berries. A favorite treat is slippery salmon, which they hook out of rivers with their curved claws.

A tapir uses its lifted trunk like a snorkel
as it swims through forest rivers and pools.

Malayan tapir, Southeast Asia

Tapir

Large, leaf-shaped footprints on the rain-forest floor will lead you to a tapir. You have to tread quietly though, since this mammal is extremely shy. Although it can be as large as a donkey, it needs to hide from big cats— its main predators.

The tapir has a long nose, a bit like an elephant's trunk, which it uses to pick fruits and leaves to eat. When it needs to cool off, it finds some gloopy mud to lie in. Baby tapirs look very different from their parents. They have a pattern of pale spots and stripes that helps them hide among patches of shadow and sunlight in the forest.

Saiga

Somewhere, out in the sea of golden grass, the saigas are hiding. These weird-looking animals live on vast plains, called steppes, which stretch across the center of Asia. It's hard to spot their herds, because they are always on the move. Each year, saigas travel huge distances in search of fresh grass to eat. Only the male saiga has horns; however, both males and females have huge, droopy noses. This stretched snout helps the saiga control its body temperature by warming the air it breathes in or cooling its blood.

There used to be millions of saigas, but hunting by humans reduced their population to the thousands. Now, the species is protected and there are many more, although it is still endangered.

When it is just two days old, a saiga calf can already run faster than a human!

Saiga, Central Asia

Glossary

alga Simple, plantlike life-form mostly found in water, including the ocean. Algae can be tiny and too small for us to see, or very large, such as seaweeds.

amphibian Animal with a backbone that usually spends part of its life in water and the rest on land. It usually develops from an egg to a larva, and then into an adult. Frogs and newts are examples of amphibians.

bulb Fat, fleshy part of some plants that is buried underground and acts as a food store.

camouflage Color or pattern that disguises an animal where it lives, to help it hide from attackers.

carnivorous Description of organisms that eat meat.

cell Smallest building block from which a living thing is made. Some tiny life-forms have only a single cell, such as bacteria, many algae, and amebas. Large animals or plants may have trillions of cells.

conifer Tree with thin, needlelike leaves and tough cones that contain seeds. Most conifers keep their needles all year round. Fir and pine trees are conifers.

coral reef Habitat found mainly in warm, shallow seas. It is made from the rock-hard skeletons of billions of tiny animals, called corals.

crystal Shape and structure in which a mineral grows.

echolocation Using sound to figure out how far away an object is by listening for the echo from a call. Dolphins and many bats use echolocation to find their way around and to identify food.

element Basic substance from which everything is made, including living things and objects. Elements can be solid, liquid, or gas, and they may change between these different states. Oxygen, iron, carbon, and gold are all examples of elements.

endangered When an animal becomes very rare in the wild. If we do not do something to help, the animal might disappear forever and become extinct.

fossil Hardened remains of organisms that lived millions of years ago. Fossils can be of body parts, such as bones, or things made by life-forms, such as footprints.

frond Leaf of a fern. It often has delicate, feathery edges.

fungus Life-form that usually feeds on rotting or dead things. Mushrooms and mold are fungi.

gemstone Precious stone or piece of rock that has been cut and polished to make it shine.

gills Organs used to breathe underwater. Fish, crabs, lobsters, shrimp, and some amphibians have gills.

habitat Place where animals, plants, and other living things are found. Habitats can be on land or in water. Many species live only in a particular habitat.

igneous rock Rock made from cooling hot, liquid magma inside the Earth, or lava that has erupted from volcanoes.

insect Animal with three pairs of legs and a body in three sections. These are the head, the thorax (in the middle), and the abdomen (at the back). Many insects also have two pairs of wings.

invertebrate Animal with no backbone, such as insects, spiders, crabs, and lobsters.

lungs Organs used to breathe air on land.

mammal Animal with a backbone, which has warm blood, and fur or hair. Nearly all mammals give birth to live young, although some unusual species lay eggs. All mother mammals feed their young milk.

metamorphic rock Rock made from another rock under massive heat and pressure, often deep underground.

meteorite Chunk of rock that has traveled through space and crashed into a planet, such as the Earth.

microscope Scientific instrument that magnifies objects, allowing us to see things too small for our eyes. They can have a camera to take images of microscopic life.

microscopic Description of something that can only be seen clearly by humans with the help of a microscope.

migration Long journey made by animals to find a new place to feed or raise their families. Many animals migrate every year between their summer and winter homes.

mineral Solid material made of chemical elements. When different minerals are mixed together, they create rock.

mollusk Type of invertebrate with a soft body and sometimes a shell, including octopuses, clams, and snails.

myth Story or tale.

nectar Sweet, sugary liquid made by flowers. Insects, birds, and mammals visit the flowers to drink the nectar.

organic Made by a living thing.

organism Any living thing, such as a plant, animal, fungus, alga, or bacterium.

oxygen Invisible gas that animals, including humans, need to breathe. It is released by algae and plants and is one of the main gases in air. It also dissolves in water.

parasite Organism that lives on or in another host organism and causes it harm. Parasites feed on their host and cannot live without it. Examples of parasites include mosquitoes, vampire bats, some flatworms, and corpse flowers.

photosynthesis Chemical process by which plants and algae make their own food using the energy from sunlight. As they do this, they release oxygen gas.

plankton Tiny living things that drift in oceans and lakes and that are often too small for us to see. They include algae and small animals, such as shrimp and copepods.

poison Harmful substance made as a defense. Poison made by animals is often found in their skin. An attacker is poisoned if touches or eats the poisonous organism.

pollen Dustlike grains made by flowers and the cones of conifer trees. Pollen spreads on the wind, or with the help of animals. When pollen is moved from flower to flower, or cone to cone, it makes the flower or cone produce seeds.

pollination Moving pollen between plants so they can make seeds. Pollen is usually moved by wind or by animals known as pollinators.

predator Animal that hunts another animal, called prey, for food.

prehistoric From a very time long ago. Many prehistoric animals and plants no longer exist, but we know about them from fossils.

prey Animal that is hunted by a predator.

rain forest Forest habitat where it is very wet and rains a lot. The largest rain forests are in the world's hot, tropical areas, and their trees can be very tall. They are home to huge numbers of different plants and animals.

reptile Animal with a backbone that has tough skin, is covered in hard scales, and usually lays eggs. Reptiles include snakes, lizards, turtles, and crocodiles.

resin Thick yellow, brown, or red liquid produced by trees. It oozes out of cuts in bark to help the wound close.

rock Hard solid made from minerals.

sap Sugary liquid produced by plants. It moves around inside stems and branches, a bit like blood in animals.

seaweed Type of large alga that grows in the ocean. Seaweeds photosynthesize like plants.

sedimentary rock Rock made when sand, gravel, and other pieces of rock pile up and are squashed together.

species Particular type of animal, plant, or other living thing. For example, the lion and cheetah are different species of cat. Members of the same species can breed together to produce young, but they usually cannot breed with other species.

spore Dustlike grains released by ferns, mosses, and fungi, which will grow into a new organism.

ultraviolet light Type of light invisible to us, but which can be seen by some other animals. Some minerals glow under ultraviolet (UV) light. UV light is what makes human skin tan, and, unless we protect ourselves, it can cause sunburn.

vein Long tube or pipe that carries liquid in an animal or plant. In animals, veins carry blood. Plant veins transport water and sugar.

venom Harmful liquid made by an animal. Venom is different from poison, because it is delivered by stingers or a bite into prey or an attacker's body.

Visual guide

Gold, page 6
Group: Element
Mohs hardness: 2.5-3
Made from: Gold

Gypsum desert rose, page 8
Group: Mineral
Mohs hardness: 2
Made from: Calcium, sulfur, oxygen, and water

Malachite, page 10
Group: Mineral
Mohs hardness: 3.5-4
Made from: Copper, carbon, oxygen, and hydrogen

Fluorite, page 12
Group: Mineral
Mohs hardness: 4
Made from: Calcium and fluorine

Precious opal, page 14
Group: Mineral
Mohs hardness: 5-6
Made from: Silicon, oxygen, and water

Turquoise, page 16
Group: Mineral
Mohs hardness: 5-6
Made from: Copper, aluminum, potassium, oxygen, hydrogen, and water

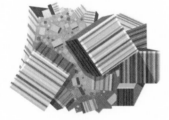

Pyrite, page 18
Group: Mineral
Mohs hardness: 6-6.5
Made from: Iron and sulfur

Ruby, page 20
Group: Mineral
Mohs hardness: 9
Made from: Aluminum and oxygen

Pumice, page 22
Group: Igneous rock
Made from: Glass

Sandstone, page 24
Group: Sedimentary rock
Made from: Quartz and feldspar

Marble, page 26
Group: Metamorphic rock
Made from: Calcite

Ammonite, page 28
Group: Fossil
Location: Worldwide

Amber, page 30
Group: Organic mineral
Made from: Resin

Emiliania coccolithophore, page 34
Emiliania huxleyi
Group: Coccolithophores
Width: 0.0004 in (0.01 mm)
Location: Worldwide

Giant kelp, page 36
Macrocystis pyrifera
Group: Brown algae
Length: 150 ft (45 m)
Location: Worldwide

Diatom, page 38
Aulacodiscus oregonus
Group: Diatoms
Width: 0.004 in (0.1 mm)
Location: Worldwide

Sea sparkle, page 40
Noctiluca scintillans
Group: Dinoflagellates
Width: 0.02 in (0.5 mm)
Location: Worldwide

Radiolarian, page 42
Saturnulus planetes
Group: Radiolarians
Width: 0.008 in (0.2 mm)
Location: Worldwide

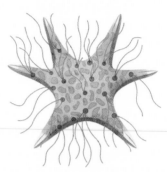

Japanese star sand, page 44
Baculogypsina sphaerulata
Group: Foraminifera
Width: 0.06 in (1.5 mm)
Location: Western Pacific Ocean

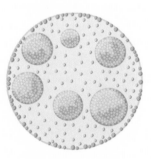

Golden volvox, page 46
Volvox aureus
Group: Green algae
Width: 0.04 in (1 mm)
Location: Worldwide

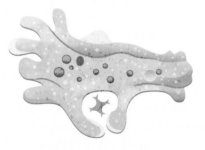

Proteus ameba, page 48
Amoeba proteus
Group: Protozoa
Length: 0.01 in (0.3 mm)
Location: Worldwide

Fly agaric, page 50
Amanita muscaria
Group: Fungi
Height: 12 in (30 cm)
Location: Worldwide

Reindeer moss, page 52
Cladonia rangiferina
Group: Green algae and fungi
Height: 4 in (10 cm)
Location: The Arctic

Water bear, page 54
Paramacrobiotus craterlaki
Group: Invertebrates
Length: 0.06 in (1.5 mm)
Location: Worldwide

Temora copepod, page 56
Temora stylifera
Group: Invertebrates
Length: 0.06 in (1.4 mm)
Location: Atlantic Ocean

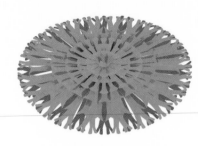

Common liverwort, page 60
Marchantia polymorpha
Group: Liverworts
Length: 4 in (10 cm)
Location: Europe

Dinosaur plant, page 62
Selaginella lepidophylla
Group: Club mosses
Height: 2 in (5 cm)
Location: Southern North America

Soft tree fern, page 64
Dicksonia antarctica
Group: Ferns
Height: 50 ft (15 m)
Location: Australia

Ginkgo, page 66
Ginkgo biloba
Group: Ginkgos
Height: 165 ft (50 m)
Location: China

Giant sequoia, page 68
Sequoiadendron giganteum
Group: Conifers
Height: 312 ft (95 m)
Location: Western
North America

Amazon water lily, page 70
Victoria amazonica
Group: Flowering plants
Leaf width: 10 ft (3 m)
Location: Northern
South America

**Southern magnolia,
page 72**
Magnolia grandiflora
Group: Flowering plants
Height: 100 ft (30 m)
Location: Southeast
North America

Tiger lily, page 74
Lilium lancifolium
Group: Flowering plants
Height: 7 ft (2 m)
Location: Asia

Large duck orchid, page 76
Caleana major
Group: Flowering plants
Height: 20 in (50 cm)
Location: Australia

Netted iris, page 78
Iris reticulata
Group: Flowering plants
Height: 6 in (15 cm)
Location: Western Asia

Dragon's blood tree, page 80
Dracaena cinnabari
Group: Flowering plants
Height: 33 ft (10 m)
Location: Socotra island off Yemen

Coconut palm, page 82
Cocos nucifera
Group: Flowering plants
Height: 100 ft (30 m)
Location: Pacific and Indian Ocean coasts

Traveler's tree, page 84
Ravenala madagascariensis
Group: Flowering plants
Height: 65 ft (20 m)
Location: Madagascar

Tank bromeliad, page 86
Neoregelia cruenta
Group: Flowering plants
Height: 18 in (45 cm)
Location: Brazil

Papyrus sedge, page 88
Cyperus papyrus
Group: Flowering plants
Height: 15 ft (4.5 m)
Location: Africa

Moso bamboo, page 90
Phyllostachys edulis
Group: Flowering plants
Height: 92 ft (28 m)
Location: China

Arctic poppy, page 92
Papaver radicatum
Group: Flowering plants
Height: 7 in (18 cm)
Location: The Arctic

King protea, page 94
Protea cynaroides
Group: Flowering plants
Height: 6 ft (2 m)
Location: South Africa

Common houseleek, page 96
Sempervivum tectorum
Group: Flowering plants
Height: 6 in (15 cm)
Location: Northern Africa, Europe, and western Asia

Red acacia, page 98
Vachellia seyal
Group: Flowering plants
Height: 56 ft (17 m)
Location: Africa and western Asia

Dog rose, page 100
Rosa canina
Group: Flowering plants
Height: 16 ft (5 m)
Location: Northern Africa, Europe, and western Asia

Common fig, page 102
Ficus carica
Group: Flowering plants
Height: 33 ft (10 m)
Location: Western Asia

Stinging nettle, page 104
Urtica dioica
Group: Flowering plants
Height: 6½ ft (2 m)
Location: Northern Africa, Europe, and Asia

Red mangrove, page 106
Rhizophora mangle
Group: Flowering plants
Height: 115 ft (35 m)
Location: Worldwide tropical coasts

Giant granadilla, page 108
Passiflora quadrangularis
Group: Flowering plants
Height: 50 ft (15 m)
Location: South America

Corpse flower, page 110
Rafflesia arnoldii
Group: Flowering plants
Flower width: 3 ft (1 m)
Location: Southeast Asia

Yellow gum, page 112
Eucalyptus leucoxylon
Group: Flowering plants
Height: 100 ft (30 m)
Location: Australia

Sugar maple, page 114
Acer saccharum
Group: Flowering plants
Height: 150 ft (45 m)
Location: North America

Grandidier's baobab, page 116
Adansonia grandidieri
Group: Flowering plants
Height: 100 ft (30 m)
Location: Madagascar

Common sundew, page 118
Drosera rotundifolia
Group: Flowering plants
Height: 8 in (20 cm)
Location: North America, Europe, and Asia

Tropical pitcher plant, page 120
Nepenthes truncata
Group: Flowering plants
Height: 16 in (40 cm)
Location: Southeast Asia

Summer cypress, page 122
Bassia scoparia
Group: Flowering plants
Height: 12 in (30 cm)
Location: Europe and Asia

Karas Mountains living stone, page 124
Lithops karasmontana
Group: Flowering plants
Height: 2 in (4 cm)
Location: Southern Africa

Saguaro, page 126
Carnegiea gigantea
Group: Flowering plants
Height: 40 ft (12 m)
Location: Southern North America, and Central America

Ghost plant, page 128
Monotropa uniflora
Group: Flowering plants
Height: 12 in (30 cm)
Location: North America, Central America, and Asia

Common sunflower, page 130
Helianthus annuus
Group: Flowering plants
Height: 10 ft (3 m)
Location: North, Central, and South America

Common dandelion, page 132
Taraxacum officinale
Group: Flowering plants
Height: 20 in (50 cm)
Location: Europe and Asia

Sea holly, page 134
Eryngium maritimum
Group: Flowering plants
Height: 24 in (60 cm)
Location: Europe

Azure vase sponge, page 138
Callyspongia plicifera
Group: Invertebrates
Height: 11 in (27 cm)
Location: The Bahamas

Torch coral, page 140
Euphyllia glabrescens
Group: Invertebrates
Width: 28 in (70 cm)
Location: Indian and Pacific Oceans

Portuguese man-of-war, page 142
Physalia physalis
Group: Invertebrates
Tentacle length: 65 ft (20 m)
Location: Worldwide tropical oceans

Tiger flatworm, page 144
Pseudoceros dimidiatus
Group: Invertebrates
Length: 3 in (8 cm)
Location: Indian and Pacific Oceans

Christmas tree worm, page 146
Spirobranchus giganteus
Group: Invertebrates
Height: 2 in (6 cm)
Location: Worldwide tropical oceans

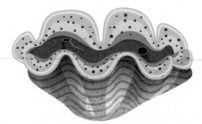

Small giant clam, page 148
Tridacna maxima
Group: Invertebrates
Length: 12 in (30 cm)
Location: Indian and Pacific Oceans

Painted snail, page 150
Polymita picta
Group: Invertebrates
Shell width: 0.8 in (2 cm)
Location: Eastern Cuba

Chambered nautilus, page 152
Nautilus pompilius
Group: Invertebrates
Length: 8 in (20 cm)
Location: Indian and Pacific Oceans

Cobalt blue tarantula, page 154
Cyriopagopus lividum
Group: Invertebrates
Legspan: 5 in (13 cm)
Location: Southeast Asia

Bumblebee millipede, page 156
Anadenobolus monilicornis
Group: Invertebrates
Length: 4 in (10 cm)
Location: Caribbean

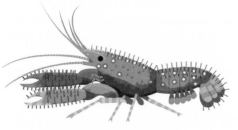

Red reef lobster, page 158
Enoplometopus occidentalis
Group: Invertebrates
Length: 4 in (10 cm)
Location: Indian and Pacific Oceans

Buff-tailed bumblebee, page 160
Bombus terrestris
Group: Invertebrates
Length: ¾ in (1.7 cm)
Location: Northern Africa, Europe, and western Asia

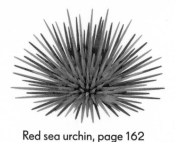

Red sea urchin, page 162
Mesocentrotus franciscanus
Group: Invertebrates
Width: 8 in (20 cm)
Location: Pacific Ocean

Whale shark, page 164
Rhincodon typus
Group: Fish
Length: 33 ft (10 m)
Location: Worldwide

Longspine porcupine fish, page 166
Diodon holocanthus
Group: Fish
Length: 20 in (50 cm)
Location: Worldwide tropical oceans

Eastern newt, page 168
Notophthalmus viridescens
Group: Amphibians
Length: 6 in (14 cm)
Location: Eastern North America

Wallace's flying frog, page 170
Rhacophorus nigropalmatus
Group: Amphibians
Length: 4 in (10 cm)
Location: Southeast Asia

False map turtle, page 172
Graptemys pseudogeographica
Group: Reptiles
Length: 10 in (25 cm)
Location: US

Equatorial anole, page 174
Anolis aequatorialis
Group: Reptiles
Length: 8 in (20 cm)
Location: Northwest South America

Eastern diamondback rattlesnake, page 176
Crotalus adamanteus
Group: Reptiles
Length: 6 ft (1.8 m)
Location: Southeastern US

Gharial, page 178
Gavialis gangeticus
Group: Reptiles
Length: 16 ft (5 m)
Location: Southern Asia

Southern cassowary, page 180
Casuarius casuarius
Group: Birds
Height: 6 ft (1.7 m)
Location: Southeast Asia and Australia

King eider, page 182
Somateria spectabilis
Group: Birds
Length: 25 in (63 cm)
Location: The Arctic

Victoria crowned pigeon, page 184
Goura victoria
Group: Birds
Length: 29 in (74 cm)
Location: Northern New Guinea

Black heron, page 186
Egretta ardesiaca
Group: Birds
Length: 26 in (66 cm)
Location: Africa

Bald eagle, page 188
Haliaeetus leucocephalus
Group: Birds
Length: 3 ft (1 m)
Location: North America

Acorn woodpecker, page 190
Melanerpes formicivorus
Group: Birds
Length: 9 in (23 cm)
Location: Southern North America, Central America, and northern South America

Southern masked weaver, page 192
Ploceus velatus
Group: Birds
Length: 5 in (13 cm)
Location: Southern Africa

Short-beaked echidna, page 194
Tachyglossus aculeatus
Group: Mammals
Length: 18 in (45 cm)
Location: New Guinea and Australia

Common wombat, page 196
Vombatus ursinus
Group: Mammals
Length: 4 ft (1.1 m)
Location: Southeast Australia

Brazilian three-banded armadillo, page 198
Tolypeutes tricinctus
Group: Mammals
Length: 13 in (32 cm)
Location: Brazil

West Indian manatee, page 200
Trichechus manatus
Group: Mammals
Length: 13 ft (3.9 m)
Location: Caribbean and northern coast of South America

Chimpanzee, page 202
Pan troglodytes
Group: Mammals
Length: 3ft (1 m)
Location: Central and western Africa

Long-eared myotis, page 204
Myotis evotis
Group: Mammals
Length: 4 in (10 cm)
Location: Western North America

Jaguar, page 206
Panthera onca
Group: Mammals
Length: 8 ft (2.5 m)
Location: Southern North America, Central America, and northern South America

Brown bear, page 208
Ursus arctos
Group: Mammals
Length without tail: 9 ft (2.8 m)
Location: Northern North America, Europe, and Asia

Malayan tapir, page 210
Tapirus indicus
Group: Mammals
Length: 10 ft (3 m)
Location: Southeast Asia

Saiga, page 212
Saiga tatarica
Group: Mammals
Length without tail: 5 ft (1.5 m)
Location: Central Asia

Project editor Olivia Stanford
Senior art editor Elle Ward
Designer Bettina Myklebust Stovne
US Senior editor Shannon Beatty
US Editor Margaret Parrish
Additional editing Satu Fox,
Kathleen Teece, Sally Beets
Additional design Jaileen Kaur
Jacket co-ordinator Issy Walsh
Senior jacket designer Elle Ward
Pre-production producer Dragana Puvacic
Producer Basia Ossowska
Project picture researcher Sakshi Saluja
DTP Designer Nand Kishor Acharya
Managing editor Laura Gilbert
Managing art editor Diane Peyton Jones
Delhi team head Malavika Talukder
Creative director Helen Senior
Publishing director Sarah Larter

Biology consultant Derek Harvey
Minerals consultant Dr. Devin Dennie

First American Edition, 2019
Published in the United States by DK Publishing
1450 Broadway, Suite 801, New York, NY 10018

Copyright © 2019 Dorling Kindersley Limited
DK, a Division of Penguin Random House LLC
19 20 21 22 23 10 9 8 7 6 5 4 3 2 1
001–314599–Sept/2019

A catalog record for this book
is available from the Library of Congress.
ISBN 978-1-4654-8536-6

DK books are available at special discounts when purchased in bulk for sales promotions, premiums, fund-raising, or educational use. For details, contact: DK Publishing Special Markets, 1450 Broadway, Suite 801, New York, NY 10018
SpecialSales@dk.com

Printed and bound in China

A WORLD OF IDEAS:
SEE ALL THERE IS TO KNOW

www.dk.com

224

DK would like to thank: Gary Ombler for photography; Oxford University Museum of Natural History for kindly allowing us to photograph their rocks and minerals, and Dr. Robert Knight for his assistance; Katie Lawrence and Abigail Luscombe for editorial assistance; Polly Goodman for proofreading; Daniel Long for the rocks and minerals, microscopic life, plants, and animals illustrations; Angela Rizza for the pattern and cover illustrations.

About the author: Ben Hoare has been fascinated by wildlife ever since he was a toddler. He is the features editor of a wildlife magazine and has been an editor, writer, and consultant for many DK books, including *DK findout! Birds* and the best-selling *An Anthology of Intriguing Animals*.

Picture credits

The publisher would like to thank the following for their kind permission to reproduce their photographs:
(Key: a-above; b-below/bottom; c-center; f-far; l-left; r-right; t-top)

4 Dorling Kindersley: Oxford University Museum of Natural History (tl, tc, crb, bc). **5 Alamy Stock Photo:** Susan E. Degginger (bl); PjrStudio (cl, clb); Dennis Hardley (cr); Greg C Grace (crb). **Dorling Kindersley:** Holts Gems (cla/Raw Rock Crystal, tr); Oxford University Museum of Natural History (cla, crb/Desert rose). **6-7 Dorling Kindersley:** Oxford University Museum of Natural History. **9 Dorling Kindersley:** Oxford University Museum of Natural History. **11 Getty Images:** Darrell Gulin. **12-13 Dorling Kindersley:** Oxford University Museum of Natural History (b). **14 Dorling Kindersley:** Oxford University Museum of Natural History. **16-17 Dorling Kindersley:** Oxford University Museum of Natural History (t). **18-19 Dorling Kindersley:** Oxford University Museum of Natural History. **20 Dorling Kindersley:** Oxford University Museum of Natural History. **23 Dorling Kindersley:** Oxford University Museum of Natural History. **24-25 Dorling Kindersley:** Oxford University Museum of Natural History. **26 Alamy Stock Photo:** Elena Mordasova. **28 Dorling Kindersley:** Oxford University Museum of Natural History. **31 Dorling Kindersley:** Oxford University Museum of Natural History. **32 Science Photo Library:** Dennis Kunkel Microscopy (bc); Steve Gschmeissner (clb). **33 Dreamstime.com:** Andrey Sukhachev / Nchuprin (bc). **iStockphoto.com:** micro_photo (cr). **Science Photo Library:** Dennis Kunkel Microscopy (tl); Steve Gschmeissner (crb). **34-35 Science Photo Library:** Steve Gschmeissner (b). **36-37 Getty Images:** Steven Trainoff Ph.D. **38 Science Photo Library:** Steve Gschmeissner (tl, cl, clb, bl, cr, crb); Fay Darling / Paul E Hargraves PHD (cra). **39 Science Photo Library:** Steve Gschmeissner (tr, cr, bl, br); Fay Darling / Paul E Hargraves PHD (tc). **40-41 Science Photo Library:** Gerd Guenther. **42 Science Photo Library:** Steve Gschmeissner. **45 Dreamstime.com:** Mushika. **46-47 iStockphoto.com:** micro_photo. **49 Science Photo Library:** Steve Gschmeissner. **51 Alamy Stock Photo:** Buiten-Beeld. **52 Alamy Stock Photo:** Artenex. **54 Science Photo Library:** Eye Of Science. **57 Science Photo Library:** Steve Gschmeissner. **58 Dreamstime.com:** Yap Kee Chan (ca). **59 Alamy Stock Photo:** Blickwinkel (br). **61 Alamy Stock Photo:** Andia. **63 123RF.com:** Girts Heinsbergs. **64-65 Alamy Stock Photo:** Tim Gainey. **69 iStockphoto.com:** Pgiam. **74-75 123RF.com:** Anchasa Mitchell. **76 Getty Images:** John Tiddy / Nature Picture Library. **78-79 Alamy Stock Photo:** Jada Images. **80-81 Getty Images:** Pixelchrome Inc. **82-83 iStockphoto.com:** Phetphu. **84 Alamy Stock Photo:** Witthaya Khampanant. **87 Getty Images:** Wagner Campelo / Moment Open. **89 Alamy Stock Photo:** Manfred Ruckszio. **90 Science Photo Library:** Martyn F. Chillmaid. **92 Alamy Stock Photo:** Life on white (br). **Getty Images:** 1bluecanoe / Moment Open (cr); F. Lukasseck / Radius Images (bl). **93 Alamy Stock Photo:** imageBROKER (r); Tiberius Photography (fbl); Irina Vareshina (bl); Julie Pigula (bc). **94 Dreamstime.com:** Poop. **96 Dreamstime.com:** Erika Kirkpatrick (cr); Fabrizio Troiani (bc). **GAP Photos:** Annaick Guitteny (clb). **97 Alamy Stock Photo:** Bob Gibbons (tr); Organica (cr). **Dreamstime.com:** Chuyu (b). **98-99 Alamy Stock Photo:** Rz_Botanical_Images. **100-101 Alamy Stock Photo:** imageBROKER. **102 Alamy Stock Photo:** Reda &Co Srl. **105 Alamy Stock Photo:** Nature Picture Library. **106-107 Dreamstime.com:** Seadam (c). **108 Getty Images:** Paul Starosta / Corbis. **109 Getty Images:** Paul Starosta / Corbis. **111 Alamy Stock Photo:** Biosphoto. **112 Alamy Stock Photo:** Robert Wyatt. **115 Alamy Stock Photo:** George Ostertag. **116-117 FLPA:** Ingo Arndt / Minden Pictures. **118 Getty Images:** Gerhard Schulz / The Image Bank. **122-123 Dreamstime.com:** Watcharapong Thawornwichian. **126-127 Dreamstime.com:** David Hayes. **128 Alamy Stock Photo:** Scott Camazine. **130 Getty Images:** Gary Wilkinson / Moment Open. **132-133 Getty Images:** assalve / E+. **134-135 SuperStock:** E.a. Janes / Age Fotostock. **136 123RF.com:** Anan Kaewkhammul / anankkml (tr). **Dorling Kindersley:** E. J. Peiker (cla). **Dreamstime.com:** Torsten Velden / Tvelden (clb). **Getty Images:** Bob Jensen / 500Px Plus (cl). **137 Dorling Kindersley:** Peter Janzen (c); Linda Pitkin (crb). **138 FLPA:** Norbert Wu / Minden Pictures. **141 Alamy Stock Photo:** Tyler Fox. **142 Alamy Stock Photo:** Nature Picture Library (c). **144-145 Getty Images:** Darlyne A. Murawski. **147 Alamy Stock Photo:** WaterFrame (c). **148 Alamy Stock Photo:** Liquid-Light Underwater Photography. **150 naturepl.com:** Ingo Arndt (c). **151 naturepl.com:** Ingo Arndt (cla, cr). **SuperStock:** Ingo Arndt / Minden Pictures (ca). **153 Getty Images:** Joel Sartore, National Geographic Photo Ark. **154-155 Dorling Kindersley:** Liberty's Owl, Raptor and Reptile Centre, Hampshire, UK. **156-157 Getty Images:** Joel Sartore, National Geographic Photo Ark. **158-159 Getty Images:** Dave Fleetham. **160-161 Dorling Kindersley:** Jerry Young. **162 Dreamstime.com:** Mikhail Blajenov. **164-165 Getty Images:** Torstenvelden. **166-167 Alamy Stock Photo:** WaterFrame. **168-169 naturepl.com:** MYN / JP Lawrence. **170 FLPA:** Chien Lee / Minden Pictures. **173 Getty Images:** Paul Starosta. **174-175 Getty Images:** Karine Aigner. **176-177 Alamy Stock Photo:** Nature Picture Library. **178-179 Getty Images:** Paul Starosta. **181 Getty Images:** Mark Newman. **182-183 Alamy Stock Photo:** All Canada Photos. **184 Getty Images:** Picture by Tambako the Jaguar. **186-187 SuperStock:** Seraf van der Putten / Minden Pictures. **188-189 Andy Morffew. 191 Alamy Stock Photo:** William Leaman. **192 Getty Images:** Catherina Unger. **194-195 Getty Images:** Joel Sartore, National Geographic Photo Ark. **197 SuperStock:** Juergen & Christine Sohns / Minden Pictures. **198 Alamy Stock Photo:** BIOSPHOTO. **200-201 Getty Images. 203 Dreamstime.com:** Patricia North. **204-205 Getty Images:** Michael Durham / Minden Pictures. **206-207 Getty Images:** Fuse. **209 Getty Images:** Joel Sartore, National Geographic Photo Ark. **210-211 Getty Images:** Joel Sartore. **212 123RF.com:** Victor Tyakht. **Cover images: Front: Alamy Stock Photo:** Blickwinkel ca/ (Weaver), imageBROKER cr, Manfred Ruckszio cla; **Dorling Kindersley:** Natural History Museum, London ca/ (Opal), Oxford University Museum of Natural History crb/ (Turquoise); **Getty Images:** Joel Sartore, National Geographic Photo Ark cla/ (Echidna), clb, Darlyne A. Murawski crb, Stephen Dalton / Minden Pictures cb; **Science Photo Library:** Steve Gschmeissner ca

All other images © Dorling Kindersley. For further information see: www.dkimages.com